Dividing and Uniting Germany

Dividing and Uniting Germany is a concise introduction to the process which led to the division of Germany in 1949, and its unification in 1990. While Germany is now politically united, it is still economically, socially and culturally deeply divided along the east–west axis, and this book also explores these problems facing post-unification Germany.

Dividing and Uniting Germany examines all the key issues, including:

- the role of the Allies in the post-war division of Germany, and the question of blame for the division
- the integration of West and East Germany into their respective blocks
- the process of unification in 1990
- the problems of integrating east and west after 1990
- Germany's Nazi and socialist past
- the move towards the 'Berlin Republic'.

Dividing and Uniting Germany provides an essential and original introduction to the challenges which Germany faced in its recent past and the problems still confronting it today.

J. K. A. Thomaneck is Professor of German at the University of Aberdeen. His many books include *The German Democratic Republic: Politics, Government and Society* (Berg, 1989). **Bill Niven** is Reader in German at The Nottingham Trent University.

The Making of the Contemporary World
Edited by Eric J. Evans and Ruth Henig
University of Lancaster

The Making of the Contemporary World series provides challenging interpretations of contemporary issues and debates within strongly defined historical frameworks. The range of the series is global, with each volume drawing together material from a range of disciplines – including economics, politics and sociology. The books in this series present compact, indispensable introductions for students studying the modern world.

Titles include:

The Uniting of Europe
From discord to concord
Stanley Henig

The International Economy Since 1945
Sidney Pollard

United Nations in the Contemporary World
David J. Whittaker

Latin America
John Ward

Thatcher and Thatcherism
Eric J. Evans

Decolonization
Raymond Betts

The Soviet Union in World Politics, 1945–1991
Geoffrey Roberts

China Under Communism
Alan Lawrence

The Cold War
An interdisciplinary history
David Painter

Conflict and Reconciliation in the Contemporary World
David J. Whittaker

States and Nationalism in Europe Since 1945
Malcolm Anderson

US Foreign Policy Since 1945
Alan Dobson and Steve Marsh

Women and Political Power in Europe Since 1945
Ruth Henig and Simon Henig

Communism and its Collapse
Stephen White

Forthcoming titles include:

Multinationals
Peter Wardley

Pacific Asia
Yumei Zhang

Conflicts in the Middle East Since 1945
Beverley Milton-Edwards and Peter Hinchcliffe

The Irish Question
Patrick Maume

Right Wing Extremism
Paul Hainsworth

Dividing and Uniting Germany

J. K. A. Thomaneck and Bill Niven

London and New York

First published 2001
by Routledge
11 New Fetter Lane, London EC4P 4EE

Simultaneously published in the USA and Canada
by Routledge
29 West 35th Street, New York, NY 10001

Routledge is an imprint of the Taylor & Francis Group

© 2001 J. K. A. Thomaneck and Bill Niven

Typeset in Times by
Keyword Typesetting Services, Wallington, Surrey
Printed and bound in Great Britain by
TJ International Ltd, Padstow, Cornwall

British Library Cataloguing in Publication Data
A catalogue record for this book is available from the British
Library

Library of Congress Cataloging in Publication Data
Niven, Bill, 1956–
  Dividing and uniting Germany / Bill Niven and
J. K. A. Thomaneck.
    p. cm – (The making of the contemporary world)
  Includes bibliographical references and index.
    1. German reunification question (1949–1990) 2. Germany –
History – Unification, 1990 – Social aspects. 3. Regionalism –
Germany. I. Thomaneck, Jürgen. II. Title. III. Series
  DD257.25.N58 2000
  943.087–dc21   00-032319

ISBN 0-415-18328-6 (hbk)
ISBN 0-415-18329-4 (pbk)

Contents

Abbreviations   *vii*

Maps   *ix*

1   The state of the nation   1

2   The division of Germany   11

3   The two German states: realities and images   31

4   The intervening years: long-term factors in change   42

5   The events of 1989/1990   57

6   Unification?   68

7   Coming to terms with the past   79

8   Germany into the new millennium   90

Bibliography   95

Index   101

Abbreviations

CDU   Christian Democratic Union
COMECON   Council for Mutual Economic Assistance
CPSU   Communist Party of the Soviet Union
CSCE   Conference on Security and Cooperation in Europe
CSU   Christian Social Union
DBD   Democratic Farmers' Party of Germany
DSU   German Social Union
DVU   German People's Union
ECSC   European Coal and Steel Community
EEC   European Economic Community
EU   European Union
FDGB   Free German Trade Union
FDP   Free Democratic Party
FRG   Federal Republic of Germany
GDR   German Democratic Republic
IFM   The Initiative for Peace and Human Rights
KPD   Communist Party of Germany
LDPD   Liberal Democratic Party of Germany
NATO   North Atlantic Treaty Organisation
NDPD   National Democratic Party of Germany
NSDAP   National Socialist German Workers' Party
OEEC   Organization for European Economic Cooperation
PDS   Party of Democratic Socialism (successor to SED)
SED   Socialist Unity Party
SMA   Soviet Military Administration
SPD   Social Democratic Party
UNESCO   United Nations Educational, Scientific and Cultural
   Organization
VdgB   Farmers' Mutual Aid Association
WEU   Western European Union

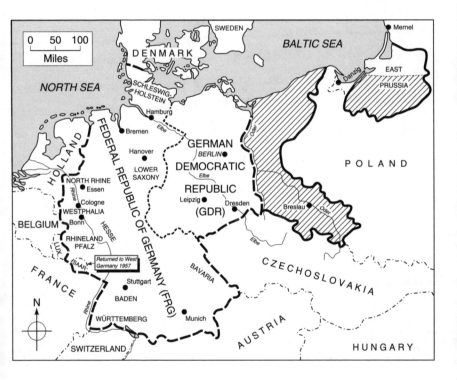

Map 1 Germany divided (1949).

Map 2 United Germany showing the *Länder* and the former German–German border.

1 The state of the nation

A DIVIDED UNITED GERMANY

On 3 October 1990, West Germany (the Federal Republic of Germany, or FRG) and East Germany (the German Democratic Republic, or GDR) were united, and thus the year 2000 marks the tenth anniversary of unification. Nationwide celebrations are already being planned. Yet 10 years after unification the new Germany is still socially, economically and politically a deeply divided country. Politicians of all colours in Germany have acknowledged this issue, but have come up with different interpretations. At the far-left of the political spectrum, the PDS (Party of Democratic Socialism, successor-party to the GDR's Socialist Unity Party or SED) has vehemently blamed west German arrogance and dominance. At the other end of the political spectrum, the right-wing CDU (Christian Democratic Party) has sought to explain the rift by pointing to the ruinous economic and moral legacy of socialism.

The symptoms of this east–west divide are manifold. Demographically, there is a clear demarcation between the 'old' and 'new' *Länder*. The latter are affected by a continuous loss of population. In 1998 alone, 160,000 people left the eastern part. With the exception of Saxony, the east has the lowest population density in Germany. It has the sharpest division between town and country; it is the most rural part and has the highest percentage of people working in agriculture. With the exception of the western part of Berlin, the eastern *Länder* boast the lowest numbers of foreigners, i.e. guest workers, asylum seekers, and other minor categories of immigrants. Social strata structures in east and west are markedly different. Individual property ownership is unevenly distributed between the old and the new *Länder*. More east Germans are employed in low-paid jobs, and there is an east–west divide in respect of unemployment. The eastern unemployment figure tends to be between 7 per cent and 9 per cent higher. According to a government report of 1998, 22 per cent of children in east Germany live in poverty, as opposed to 12 per cent in the west. There is a clear difference between east and west in respect of expenditure on leisure activities, with people in the east spending 20 per cent less; this reflects the lower income levels there. With the exception of Bremen and the Saarland, the eastern *Länder* are also the least popular parts of Germany for holidays. Altogether, Germany displays the economic characteristics of the Italian *mezzogiorno* on an east–west axis. The gross domestic product is lower in all eastern *Länder*.

Other areas of societal life display the same divisions. Crime figures, for instance, are much higher in the east, as are road deaths. Participation in clubs, sport and leisure organizations is lower in the east, as are church membership and political party membership. Even football is affected. Eastern German football clubs are struggling, and to date the eastern *Länder* have only one representative in the German Premier League, namely Hansa Rostock.

COMPETING CONSTRUCTIONS

What is the source of this east–west split? On one level, the dichotomy can be seen as an expression of historically divergent cultural identities. The precondition for this divergent development was the division of Germany into four occupation zones in 1945, and subsequently into two states in 1949. The main factor in this development was the socialist system in the east, and the capitalist system in the west. Even a life lived in opposition to socialism in the east, or in dissatisfaction with capitalism in the west, produced citizens who would not automatically have felt at home in the other system. The fact that the two Germanys were at the fault-line of the global east–west divide, and yet strongly linked historically, culturally, emotionally and not least personally through family ties, resulted in a mixture of mutual attraction and mutual distrust whose complex and ambivalent psychological repercussions did not end with the collapse of the Berlin Wall.

This historical dichotomy has been overlaid and arguably enhanced by developments since 1989/1990. First, the process of unification itself was essentially unequal, the West Germans having more say than the East Germans, who, it can fairly be stated, acceded to the Federal system in almost every aspect. Second, the post-unification period witnessed the actual or perceived declassification of east Germans

either as a result of mass unemployment and economic disenfranch-
isement, or as a result of moral condemnation for their past.
According to historian Peter Bender, unification is a misnomer
because it can *per definitionem* only be between equals. What has
happened since 1989, Bender argues, has been a process of incorpora-
tion and of economic, social, and psychological expropriation on the
basis of political power politics. The unification process ignored the
personal and social history of the people in the east, which was unable
to contribute to the new Germany (Bender 1998b). Third, there is the
problem of the 'loser–winner' schism. 1990 seemed to signify the triumph of western liberalism over socialism. This sense of being the
'winners of history' is reflected in the arrogant behaviour of many
west Germans or *Wessis*. Equally, the diffidence and self-doubt of
many east Germans or *Ossis* are not the ideal psychological prerequi-
sites for handling the west Germans.

Divergence between east and west has been a matter of intense
political analysis. Thus it has been argued that the unification of
Germany took place at the end of modernity, and that post-1990
Germany reflects the multi-faceted nature of the post-modern age,
with divergence and plurality mapping particularly on the east–west
axis. Assessing the east German consciousness, west German journal-
ist Michael Rutschky argues that it is only now, 10 years after the
rejection of the GDR by its citizens, that a 'real-existing' separate
consciousness has evolved (Rutschky 1995). It is not to be defined as
a continuing or belated negative GDR patriotism, nor as an outcome
of feelings of inferiority as second-class citizens in the German economic miracle (*Wirtschaftswunder*). Rather it is to be defined on the
basis of free choice. Whereas in the GDR people had no option, they
can now freely and deliberately choose an eastern German consciousness in opposition to the western German hegemony of capitalist
prosperity. Rutschky describes eastern Germany as a firmed-up,
(self-)conscious province inside Germany. It has only now had the
opportunity to come into existence because nobody is forced to live
there. Staying there is therefore voluntary. Germany is being enriched
by another form of regionalism.

Against this it must be said that what the new Germany is witnes-
sing is a qualitatively new type of regionalism inside one country.
Whereas traditionally region and regionalism are defined on the
basis of geographical, functional, social, cultural, linguistic and historical criteria, where regions might have administrative (sometimes only
partial) autonomy, and where that might also generate regional patriotism, the situation in the new Germany is very different. Regions such

as Bavaria, Schleswig-Holstein, or Baden are defined along such traditional lines. The new *Länder* individually can perhaps also be defined
in terms of traditional criteria, with the exception of Western
Pomerania, now an adjunct to Mecklenburg, and Berlin, now separated from Brandenburg, historically its traditional hinterland. But, by
and large, the new east German regionalism cuts across such lines.
Uniquely, this regionalism has grown out of a rejected ideological
construct imposed during the Cold War between the two power
blocs after 1945. And it is inseparably bound up with the fact of an
economic divide between east and west, eastern regionalism connoting,
often, a partly de-industrialized, semi-agriculturalized backwater
rather than anything else.

In contrast to Rutschky's theory of a freely chosen alternative identity, other critics have suggested that east German consciousness is
marked, indeed scarred, by nostalgia for the GDR (*Ostalgie*) or indeed
'eastern stubbornness' (*Osttrotz*). Rather than freely forming a new
identity, east Germans have seized on to a reconstructed image of the
GDR in answer to an increasing sense of frustration and disorienta-
tion. The image is a distortion because it conveniently excises all that
was bad about the GDR and results in an idealization. This identity
formation through imagined reconstruction of the past is also deeply
ironic, given that the GDR population never identified with their state
as much as they do now that it has gone. It is also self-deceiving, not
least because the GDR is imagined from a position of relative capitalist prosperity: 'we've got the deutschmark, you can come back now,
Erich', runs one slogan (in reference to former GDR leader Erich
Honecker). But is it all negative?

The essential conundrum is whether or not constructions of east
German identity are regarded purely as defensive reactions to insecu-
rities in the present, and therefore as a kind of cushion to fall back on,
or whether they are seen as legitimate expressions of an alternative
political and social culture. Clearly, reconstructions of the past which
result in passive and self-deluding retrospection are not positive.
However, selective reappropriations of certain arguably positive
aspects of socialist society – job security, low rents, right to a home
– need not be coupled with a total transfiguration of past realities.
Moreover, it is not just the GDR some east Germans look back on
with longing, but also the time of the 1989 revolution (*Wende*), when
they took to the streets to fight for greater freedom, and when certain
forms of basis democracy evolved which resulted in a brief period of
political influence. Two key features of east German consciousness,
then, could be a heightened sense of social justice and of political

rights. Rather than projecting these back into a lost past, many east Germans project them into a vision of a better future, so that the emphasis is forward-looking rather than backward-looking.

Support for the PDS in the new *Länder* is to an extent based on this active commitment to these key features. The Christian Democrats tend to dismiss voting for the PDS as a form of protest, equating support for the party thereby with support for the right-wing extremist DVU (German People's Union). While there may be those who vote for the PDS purely because they cannot stand the sight of capitalist west Germans, just as there are those who vote for the DVU because they cannot stand the sight of Turks, this is about as far as any legitimate comparison extends. Clearly, Turks are not to blame for present economic ills; rampant capitalism certainly is to blame for some of them. Moreover, while racism is based on discrimination and exclusion, support for the PDS is the expression of a desire to be re-included, given that unemployment and deindustrialization have led to social and political marginalization. The established west German parties, notably the CDU and CSU (Christian Social Union), may be right to suspect some PDS politicians of not having the soundest of democratic credentials, but one might equally suspect the CDU and CSU of not having the soundest motive – namely irritation at the PDS power base in the east – for pointing this out. Nor can the questionable credibility of the PDS detract from the legitimacy of its call for greater east German participation.

Wolfgang Thierse (SPD, or Social Democratic Party), an east German and current President of the *Bundestag*, has repeatedly pointed out that east Germans, because of their self-assertion during the *Wende*, are the truly revolutionary Germans. Taking this further, one might contend that west Germans had democracy imposed upon them after 1945, whereas the east Germans had to fight for it in 1989/1990. While what the west Germans have learnt to respect after decades of living with it and using it is parliamentary democracy, the east Germans spontaneously and voluntarily chose a form of direct democracy. In a curious inversion of Marxist theory and practice, the socialist revolution came with the collapse of socialism, and the anti-fascist self-liberation myth came true only with the demise of the system which propagated this myth.

Arguably, then, the revolutionary east Germans – i.e. not including those socialist functionaries and stalwarts whose repressive influence had rightly to be curtailed after 1990 – imported a fresh and vigorous basis-democratic consciousness into united Germany which, combined with the sense of solidarity that was built up in the face of actually existing socialism, together too with an appreciation of some of the possible virtues of GDR socialism and with a vestigial utopianism, shaped a distinct identity. It is this identity which asserts itself in the face of a capitalism whose impact, despite a limited degree of state control, subsidies and social protection, has indeed been somewhat ruthless and self-regulating. Arguably, too, only west German acceptance of this identity, indeed only a preparedness on the part of west Germans to rethink their own identity, hitherto very much based on material wealth and economic power, will help to create an overarching sense of national togetherness.

THE PHANTOM OF NATIONALISM

While the Germans have been grappling with internal problems of unification, the outside world has watched closely for signs of renascent German nationalism. The results of the regional elections in Saxony-Anhalt in April 1998 seemed to confirm worst fears of upheaval in Germany's party-political landscape: the right-wing extremist German People's Union, which had not contested an election in Saxony-Anhalt before, secured 12.9 per cent of the votes at its first attempt. The DVU's success was based entirely on its 3 million DM propaganda campaign, which had utilized some 20,000 posters and over a million targeted letters to young voters. Its slogans included 'German money for German tasks' and 'Out with foreign criminals', signalling the party's clear right-wing extremist stance in a region with the highest unemployment in Germany. Its success was an embarrassment to the established parties, and the subject of much concern in the media. Even the *Bild Zeitung* (roughly comparable with *The Sun* in the UK), renowned for its strong stance to the right of the political spectrum, stated: 'Black Sunday for the ruling coalition in Bonn. Black Sunday for all democrats'. In reference to the DVU leader Gerhard Frey, another headline ran: 'The fat man who would be Führer'.

Had Margaret Thatcher been right after all? Foreign critics of unification had expressed the fear that the Germans, released after 40 years from the grip of the respective Cold War blocs, would soon be on the rampage again, if more in the political and economic than in the military realm. Such opinions were often predicated on a more than prejudicial and self-interestedly essentialist projection of the Germans as aggressive and expansionist – witness the ridiculous complaints by a number of countries with dubious (or no) democratic credentials that Germany's post-unification foreign policy was being driven by a renewed Hitlerism. Serbia's press and politicians, from 1991 onwards, have consistently presented Germany as planning a 'Fourth Empire' from the Baltic to the Adriatic in league with Croatia and Slovenia. When, in March 1992 in reaction to Turkey's onslaught against the Kurds, Germany imposed a weapons embargo, the Turkish President Özal compared Foreign Minister Genscher to Hitler. Similar questionable instrumentalizations of the German past have come from Iran and China.

But there have also been understandable anxieties abroad, such as those of the Poles and the Czechs, who feared that a strong united Germany under the influence of the CDU might question the existing eastern borders with Poland and the Czech Republic, or at least lay some sort of claim to Silesia and the Sudetenland. Fears of a renascent violent nationalism were fuelled by attacks in Germany on foreigners, the most notorious being in Rostock in August 1992, and Mölln in November 1992, when three Turks died (bringing the total to seventeen deaths from racist attacks in 1992 alone). Such acts of murder are unforgiveable; nevertheless, it must be said that aggressive nationalist elements in German society do not command much support and certainly do not pose a significant threat to national or international stability. The fears of Poland and the Czech Republic have been allayed by the German pledge to respect the borders, by 'Friendly Neighbour' Treaties in 1991 and 1992, and by Germany's championship of the entry of east European countries into NATO and the EU. Racist attacks have largely remained sporadic and have prompted massive nationwide protest and candle-lit marches for tolerance. In the April 1999 regional elections in Hesse, the CDU was helped to power by a campaign of fomenting resentment against foreigners; but such populism has not been able to hold up Germany's new laws on citizenship, ushered in by the new SPD–Greens coalition government, which for the first time give immigrants' children born in Germany a right to a German passport: this first shift from *ius sanguinis* to *ius soli* represents an important step towards a multicultural concept of what it means to be 'German'.

POLITICAL TRENDS

In the event, the success of the DVU in Saxony-Anhalt turned out to be a flash in the pan; in subsequent 1998 regional elections in Mecklenburg-West Pomerania and Bavaria, the party failed to make any impact. It played no role in the national elections of September

1998. The point is that nationalistic excess has *not* been united Germany's problem. There have been calls for a new German pride, a less humble attitude to the past and a culture of more self-assertiveness, but this has never, except in a few cases, degenerated into simple chauvinism. Nor can these calls really catch the public imagination. As long as east and west Germans are struggling to come to terms with one another, Germany's big difficulty will not be nationalism, but achieving a coherent sense of nationhood.

A broader view of political developments over recent years underlines this interpretation. The most significant aspect of the 1998 Saxony-Anhalt elections, judged in the medium to long term, was not the success of the far right, but the fact that the SPD (which gained 35.9 per cent of the vote) formed a minority government dependent on the support and 'tolerance' of the PDS (19.6 per cent). The PDS – after years of being stigmatized by traditional west German parties as a largely unreformed offshoot of the SED – was gaining access to the corridors of power. This trend was reinforced by the regional elections in Mecklenburg-West Pomerania in September 1998. Here, as in Saxony-Anhalt, the Greens and the FDP (Free Democratic Party) failed to gain enough votes to get into the regional parliament. The outcome also confirmed the declining fortunes of the CDU (24 seats, 6 less than in 1994), and strengthened the position of the SPD (27 seats, 4 more than 1994) and PDS (20 seats, 2 more than 1994) in the new Mecklenburg-West Pomerania parliament. The resultant political stalemate as to who would form the new *Land* government was resolved in the most revolutionary manner in the history of the new Germany: the SPD and PDS formed a coalition government, leaving the CDU as the opposition party. This is the first time the PDS has been accepted as a respectable coalition partner.

The success of the PDS is a purely eastern phenomenon. This was borne out by the elections in Bavaria on 13 September 1998, where it performed miserably. It was also borne out by the national elections on 27 September 1998, when it achieved 5.1 per cent of the vote nationwide (0.7 per cent more than in 1994). 19.5 per cent of the voters in the east voted PDS, in contrast to a mere 1.1 per cent in the west. In 10 of the 71 eastern constituencies, it came second after the SPD, winning four constituencies outright, all in former East Berlin. Other east–west differences hinted at by the 1998 eastern *Länder* elections were confirmed by the national elections. While the FDP won 6.2 per cent of the vote (0.7 per cent less than 1994) and got into parliament, it obtained only 3.6 per cent of votes in the east, in contrast to 7 per cent in the west. A similar picture emerges in respect of The Greens, who secured 6.7 per cent of the nationwide vote (0.7 per cent less than in 1994). With the exception of Berlin, The Greens are not a political force anywhere in the eastern *Länder*, where they obtained only between 2.9 per cent and 4.4 per cent of the votes. In the majority of eastern constituencies, right-wing parties fared better than the FDP and The Greens, without, however, having any political impact.

The most fundamental development of the national elections was, of course, the change of government from CDU/FDP to SPD/The Greens. The SPD won 40.9 per cent of the votes (4.5 per cent more than in 1994), the CDU/CSU 35.2 per cent (6.2 per cent less). But the general party distribution pattern, with the above-mentioned differences between west and east, has a significant influence on possible government patterns at *Land* and local government level. In the western *Länder,* in the event of no party achieving an absolute majority, and apart from the possibility of the formation of a grand coalition between the two major parties, there are potential coalitions with The Greens and/or the FDP for either the CDU or the SPD: thus the regional elections in Hesse in February 1999 resulted in a shift of government from SPD/The Greens to CDU/FDP. This potential does not exist in the eastern *Länder*. Here, there is the possibility of a grand coalition between CDU and SPD (as formed in Brandenburg in September 1999), or of a PDS-tolerated SPD minority government (Saxony-Anhalt), or an SPD/PDS coalition (Mecklenburg-West Pomerania). Further coalition governments in the eastern *Länder* will provide the PDS with greater representation in Germany's Second Chamber or *Bundesrat*, thereby enhancing its role above that of a minor opposition party in the *Bundestag*. This may ensure greater discussion of east German issues at federal level; also it may serve to transport the east–west dichotomy into the very heart of German politics.

DIVISION AND UNIFICATION: PROCESSES AND IMAGES

Against the background of the current schism in Germany, this book sets out to explore some of the key causes, both past and present, of its development. Chapter 2 traces the historical roots, dealing with the division of Germany in the 1945–1955 period. On the basis of this overview, Chapter 3, 'The two German states: realities and images', directly confronts the question as to who was responsible for stages of division, and who is seen to be responsible: often two different things. The focus of Chapter 4, 'The intervening years:

long-term factors in change', is on those factors which may have contributed over time to the collapse of the GDR, such as *ostpolitik*, the opposition movement, and the failure of an adequate integration of the GDR workforce. The thesis here is that an increasing gap between rhetoric (image) and fact (reality) in the GDR contributed to its fall, and that the image of the opposition movement as being focused exclusively on reform ignores its interest in improved German–German relations. Chapter 5 then deals with the events of 1989–1990, looking at the short-term factors in change, again in terms of the increasing discrepancy in the GDR between official pronouncements and reality. Chapter 6 considers the interpretative descriptors applied to the 1989–1990 period, demonstrating that these descriptors reveal different images of the *Wende* and its aftermath. The penultimate chapter, 'Coming to terms with the past', discusses attempts in the GDR and FRG to come to terms with Nazism, and united Germany's approach to the 'twin' pasts of Nazism and Stalinism, while the final Chapter 8, 'Germany into the new millennium', provides a brief concluding overview of prognoses – images – for the future of Germany in the new millennium.

2   The division of Germany

When the battles were over in May 1945, and there was no area of German soil not occupied by foreign troops, Germany was still in a state of war with 58 countries. Three of these, however, dominated the scene: the United States, the Soviet Union and Great Britain. All three agreed on one rather primitive idea, namely that wars can occur only if there is a nation which strives for world domination. They believed that it would be enough to deprive Germany of its military, economic and political power, i.e. to demilitarize the country, dismantle its industry and act as guardians over it. What did the Allied countries agree upon in particular? Roosevelt, Churchill and Stalin met for the first time at the Conference in Teheran (28 November–1 December 1943). They agreed on the division of Germany into five parts; they also agreed on the internationalization of the Ruhr district and the Saar district, and of Hamburg and the Kiel Canal under a United Nations protectorate. Stalin demanded that the German officers' caste be destroyed. There followed the Yalta Conference of February 1945: by this time the Allied troops had entered Germany and the war had been decided. Germany from the river Oder westwards was to be split into three separate zones. Each of the three major Allied powers was to run the administration of one zone. Berlin was to be administered by their combined efforts. Subsequently, France was added as a fourth occupation power after Germany had capitulated in May 1945. It got its zone from the western part of the original American zone. France was included because the Americans considered withdrawing their troops in 1947, and Britain did not want to be the only military power left next to the Russians. The supreme political power was to be in the hands of the High Command.

At Yalta, agreement was reached on how to divide Germany into zones, although Stalin began to object to a division of Germany from now on. He argued that the Hitlers of this world come and go, but that the German people would always be there. The Soviet Union insisted that the Polish western frontier should be the Oder and Neisse rivers, given that it laid claim to the 'Curzon line' as its own western frontier, which meant shifting Poland westwards. On 7 and 8 May 1945, the unconditional surrender of Germany was signed, and 1 month later the four Allied powers formally assumed supreme authority in Germany. A Control Council consisting of the commanders-in-chief of the four zones of occupation was established to decide on questions affecting Germany as a whole.

The Potsdam Conference of July and August 1945 opened on a dissonant note when the chief executives of the United States and Great Britain were faced with a number of unilateral Soviet actions in violation of the Yalta Agreements. Of most consequence for Germany's future was the transfer to Poland of the territories east of the rivers Oder and Neisse, which the protesting Western Allies had to accept as a *fait accompli,* if not *de jure.* The Western Allies could not agree to the western river Neisse as the border; they only conceded territory east of the Oder.

Among its political principles, the joint report of the Potsdam Conference again advocated the decentralization of the political system, local self-government, and the introduction of representative structures into regional, provincial and *Land* administration. For the time being, no German central government was to be established, except for administrative departments in the field of finance, transport, communications, industry and foreign trade which would form a part of the Allied Control Council. Finally, the Potsdam Conference approved the decentralization of German industry and the huge transfer of population (i.e. some 10 million people) from the east into the remainder of Germany.

After this Conference, the rift between East and West widened gradually as the Western Allies became more aware of the expansion of Soviet power into the vacuum left by the collapse of Germany. The French, moreover, had not been a party to the Potsdam Agreements and embarked now on a policy of obstruction, largely opposing any measures that might contribute to German political, organizational, and economic unity. Under these conditions, each occupation power proceeded with the reconstruction of German governmental institutions in its own zone as it saw fit.

STRUCTURES OF ADMINISTRATION

Each zone had its commander-in-chief, but consisted of several *Länder*, which the occupation powers had created. Some of these were traditional historical units such as Schleswig-Holstein, Hamburg, Bremen, Bavaria, Thuringia, Saxony, and Saxony-Anhalt, while some had a strong historical element such as Rhineland-Palatinate, Hesse, Wurttemberg-Baden, Wurttemberg-Hohenzollern, Brandenburg, and Mecklenburg-West Pomerania. Others such as Lower Saxony and North Rhine-Westfalia were new creations altogether. Each *Land* had a separate military government under the authority of the commander-in-chief. It was not until 1946 that the formation of ministerial governments with German ministers was allowed in the *Länder*. In some *Länder* the military commander appointed a Prime Minister, though the commander retained supreme authority. Some military commanders even allowed *Land* parliaments (*Landtage*), but these had a purely advisory function.

A level beneath the military governments were the district delegates, usually officers a generation younger. The main task of these military governments was to implement the Potsdam Agreements: demilitarization, decentralization of industry, denazification, democratization and dismantling. In addition they had to ensure that the Germans did not die of starvation. They also had to build up a German administration to fulfil all these aims.

The Control Council itself was not idle: it decided on a proportional distribution of the refugees from the east, passed some labour legislation, and agreed on the abolition of the state of Prussia, which was a dead duck anyway. When the American, British and French forces agreed on 6 March 1948 to form an economic unit, the Soviet Marshall Sokolowski left the Control Council. According to one recent commentator, Sokolowski had little option, as the Americans had embarked on a policy of disenfranchising the Council (Mai 1988).

In their efforts to reconstruct a German administration, the officers at local and *Land* level were met half-way by the Germans themselves, who had taken responsibility for clearing away the ruins, finding accommodation for the homeless and for the refugees, distributing food, organizing the provision of medical care, and creating jobs. Sometimes these endeavours were supported by the Allies, who appointed mayors, as well as officials at the local, area and district level. Soon this went hand in hand with the pursuit of democratization. Political groups emerged, and the first political parties were formed in the Soviet zone. They had to be approved by the zone commander as democratic. These parties were: the Communist Party, the Social Democrats, the Christian Democrats and the Liberal Democrats. More or less the same parties were in time also allowed in the other three zones (cf. Biefang 1995). The development of central institutions inside the zones was encouraged most by the British, and least by the French, who disliked everything that smacked of German unity. They envisaged a Germany consisting of many states inside a loose federation.

In February 1946, the British military government set up an institution known as a *Zonenbeirat,* a small parliament for the whole zone with an exclusively advisory function. Its members were appointed by the military government. Members of this *Zonenbeirat* were Konrad Adenauer, West Germany's first Chancellor, and Kurt Schumacher, who was the leader of the SPD until his death in 1951. On 1 December 1946, the zonal military government delegated some of its powers to the *Länder*. The government drew up an ordinance specifying their powers. This document reserved four areas of responsibility for the military authorities or a future central government. These included matters such as foreign relations, defence, nationality issues, currency, coinage, central banking, postal and telegraphic communications, railroads and highways. The British occupation authorities were, however, not very keen to devolve any power upon German institutions, and might have put off constitutional developments and elections for several years, had not international developments in 1946 forced their hand.

Under these conditions, the first local elections in the British zone took place in September 1946, and the first *Land* elections followed in April 1947. The *Länder* of the British zone were Lower Saxony, North Rhine-Westfalia, Hamburg and Schleswig-Holstein (cf. Jürgensen 1997). The American zone comprised the *Länder* Bavaria, Wurttemberg-Baden, Hesse and Bremen. Forms of German political representation had already been reconstructed at the local, area and district level, and Bavaria even had a Prime Minister by the end of May 1945. In February 1946, a directive was issued to the Minister-Presidents ordering them to establish committees for the drafting of constitutions for the three larger *Länder*. These drafts served as a working basis for the constitutional conventions elected there by popular vote in June 1946. By October 1946, these conventions had finished their work and the constitutions were submitted to the military authorities for approval. Finally, they were ratified by the people at the same time as the new diets were elected. No sooner were the *Länder* governments in the American zone in place than the need was felt to coordinate their administrative services in inter-*Länder* matters: a Council of *Länder* was established at Stuttgart, consisting of the three Minister-Presidents and the Mayor of Bremen, with deputies and technical advisers (cf. Füssl 1995). A permanent secretariat prepared the agenda and the proposals for the weekly meetings. The French on the other hand did not tolerate such inter-*Länder* developments inside their zone. Nor did they delegate important administrative matters. They even forbade the use of D for *Deutsch* or *Deutschland* in names of parties or organizations (as in SPD).

ON THE ROAD TO WEST GERMANY

During 1946 the British and Americans became increasingly aware of Germany's political potential. They realized that a divided Germany of many small states would be useless in the new Cold War between the Soviet Union and the West. In September 1946, a number of bizonal fusion agreements between the British and American zones were signed which merged the zonal administrations for economics, food and agriculture, transport and finance. The bizonal authorities consisted of functional committees of six competent *Länder* ministers each, with all six *Länder* having an equal vote. The committees had the power to issue directives valid for the participating *Länder*, but had to rely on the cooperation of the executive departments of the *Länder*. The catastrophic deterioration in the food supply situation led to a drastic revision of the bizonal structure in June 1947. A new arrangement provided for an Economic Council to be selected by the parliaments of the various *Länder*. An Executive Committee consisting of one full-time representative from each *Land* represented the interests of the *Länder*.

Executive Directors responsible to both Economic Council and Executive Committee were to head the administrative departments. The ordinances of the Economic Council, sanctioned by the Bipartite Board of the occupation authorities, had to be implemented promptly by the *Länder*. The bizonal administration was revised in February 1948 because the first changes had not been sweeping enough to prevent irregularities. The Economic Council was enlarged and a *Länder* Council with the power to initiate bills and with rights of veto took the place of the Executive Committee. The heads of the administrative departments were combined into an Administrative Council responsible in varying degrees to the Economic Council, the military governors, and the *Länder* Council. This innovation enabled the Economic Council to force the *Länder* to comply with its directives and even to set up its own enforcement agencies. Bizonal revenues came from customs, excises, railroads, and postal services as well as a share of *Länder* income and corporation taxes. The revision also enlarged the bizonal sphere of legislative powers and reaffirmed the supremacy of bizonal over *Länder* law. A High Court and Central Bank completed the structure.

At the same time, the two Anglo-American zones and then the French zone were included in the Marshall Aid Plan. This aid programme was based on the so-called Truman doctrine. Truman, in April 1947, proclaimed the following agenda: first, Communism had to be contained and isolated; second, The United States had to utilize their riches in order to enable those nations who suffered through the war to rebuild their economy, to rid these countries of unemployment, and to raise their standard of living. The American Foreign Minister Marshall offered this aid to all European Countries, even the Communist ones. But the Soviet Union forced Poland and the CSSR to turn down the offer. 16 European nations formed the Organization for European Economic Cooperation (OEEC), the three Western zones being represented by the occupying powers.

The idea was that Western Germany be integrated into a wider European economic system, making her less dangerous politically in future. But a new German economy could not be integrated into the European economy without a German government. In November 1947, President Truman said that some form of German government had to be created; only then could responsible authorities be established with powers to deal with problems concerning the whole of Western Germany. Local administration and zonal independence were not suitable mechanisms for the integration of a huge, as yet undeveloped economy into the European economy. This was the turning-point of post-war German developments. It was as a result of the Marshall Plan, i.e. of American economic interests and American anti-communism, that Western Germany ceased to be an occupied territory and became a sovereign state. Now the theory was that Western Germany must be a strong economic power in order to save democracy. But it would also need its own political Western democratic ideology. In order to give this a proper foundation, the Germans would have to be allowed to develop their *own* political life – otherwise it would have the odium that it was forced upon them by the Western Allies.

Within this conceptual framework, political life started again in Western Germany. In July 1948, the German Minister-Presidents were asked by the three Western Allies to comply with the plan to

merge the three Western zones into one political, economic and constitutional unit. The steps to be taken were outlined in the Frankfurt
Documents, which required the Minister-Presidents to convoke a con-
stituent assembly by September 1948. The *Länder* would organize the
elections for this assembly. The assembly was to work out a democratic constitution, which would turn Western Germany into a federal
republic with a strong central government. This constitution had to be
approved by the military governors and accepted by two-thirds of the
Länder. But the third Frankfurt document also stated that the occupying countries would continue to control foreign policy, foreign trade,
reparations, decentralization of industry and de-militarization. The
Parliamentary Council met on 1 September 1948 in Bonn to work
out a constitution. This was adopted in May 1949.

The next step for the Allies was to devise a scheme giving the new
provisional state sovereignty while not conceding economic and political independence to the extent that it might feel inclined or be able to
repeat Hitler's policies. This raises the issue as to whether such a state
would in fact *be* a sovereign state. For West Germany, the situation in
1949 was as follows. It was not allowed to have its own army, to
conduct its own foreign policy, or have diplomatic relations with
any other country. The High Commission, which replaced the commanders-in-chief in representing the Allies, also retained certain rights
within West Germany. It could tap telephones, open mail, veto laws
passed by the *Bundestag* and changes to the Basic Law. It could super-
vise all administration and the economy. The occupational status
under the High Commission lasted until 23 October 1954, when the
Paris Treaties were signed.

West Germany was to be integrated into a wider European political,
military and economic system. In October 1949, it became part of the
OEEC. It joined the European Parliament in 1951. While this
Parliament was subsequently of no political importance, joining did
mean international recognition for West Germany. The Western Allies
decided in 1950 that West Germany should join NATO (founded in
1949), and in 1951 the High Commission delegated foreign policy to
the FRG. West Germany now had a foreign minister. The first one
was Chancellor Adenauer. Also in 1951, the three Western powers
declared that war had ceased between them and West Germany. In
May 1955, after the Paris Treaties had been ratified by all parliaments
involved, West Germany was a sovereign state. It had its own forces,
but they were only to be used by NATO and for NATO.

This was the beginning of the Federal Republic. It was a completely
new state, an artificial creation resulting from international political

circumstances. It needed to establish its own character, and find ways of encouraging its citizens to identify with it. Constitutional and political discourse was not the way to achieve this. German constitutional life had reached 'point zero' in May 1945 – although there were still the political traditions of pre-Hitler Germany on which reconstruction of the body politic could fall back. There were also a number of political and intellectual leaders of the Weimar Republic who had survived the Third Reich and were now rallying to rebuild society and state. Some had spent years in exile, some in concentration camps and hiding places, while others came from the ivory-tower seclusion of the German intellectual, or from the inner emigration of resignation and withdrawal from politics. The majority of people, however, were stunned by the collapse of Nazi totalitarianism and relatively unconcerned about political reconstruction. Many had never been interested in politics anyway, and were now preoccupied with the day-to-day struggle for food and shelter. While this majority failed to make its political wishes known, a very vocal minority dominated the media, which played a key role in shaping public opinion and the political scene. Within this minority, the adherents of the old Weimar Coalition – Social Democrats, left-wing liberals and left-wing Catholics - regarded the democratic traditions of the Weimar Republic as a fitting model for imitation, a model that had been betrayed by the conservative revolution.

CHANGES AND CONTINUITIES IN WEST GERMANY

This minority was also convinced, however, that parts of the Weimar Constitution might have facilitated the rise and triumph of Hitler. The Weimar Republic's parliamentary system had been based on proportional representation. As a result, many small parties had got into parliament, leading to unstable, shifting coalition governments. The provisions governing the parliamentary system of Weimar, and the emergency powers of the Reich President were adjudged to have been a serious flaw. The role and personnel of the Weimar courts (thus Hitler only got a short sentence for his attempted Putsch in 1923) came in for some strong criticism too. There was also a general belief that the extremists of both wings could have been stopped by denying them the very democratic liberties which they had abused for their assault on democracy. Some ascribed the problems of the Weimar Republic to the gradual abandonment of the German tradition of federalism. This line of attack was especially popular with spokesmen of regional sentiment in Hanover, Bavaria and the south-west. All these points of criticism played a vital part in the formulation of the elements which distinguish the Bonn Constitution from its Weimar predecessor. The question of which electoral system to choose from the two or three possibilities was extremely complex, and one in which issues of party tradition, immediate political advantage and considerations of democratic reconstruction very much intertwined. But one aspect that had exercised the best minds among previous generations of constitution-makers was not very important to the delegates in Bonn. In the 19th century and the Weimar Republic, the choice of an electoral system had usually been made with due respect to the sacrosanct character of the will of the sovereign people. The framers of the Parliamentary Council were almost exclusively concerned with the practical effects that a given electoral system might have on the electoral chances of their respective parties or on the functioning of democracy.

The critique of the Weimar system also took the form of a general criticism of 'mass democracy'. No-one could deny that Hitler's rise to power had to a large extent reflected popular preferences and followed the rules of the most democratic constitution of that age. The minority dominating the West German political scene thus felt a deep distrust of the masses and their sudden passions. The Parliamentary Council, moreover, considered it its mission to set up a constitutional democ-racy with restrictions placed upon the powers of the masses, if need be against their will. Mindful of the fact that a working majority in the *Reichstag* of the early 1930s had been rendered impossible by extreme left-wing and right-wing groupings, the framers of the Basic Law wished to prevent such negative majorities from toppling cabinets without being able to agree on a new government. They therefore introduced the 'constructive no-confidence vote' (Article 67 of the Basic Law). While the Chancellor continues to depend for tenure of office on the confidence of the lower house, he can be voted out of office only by the election of a successor. Furthermore, mindful of the abundant use of referenda in the Weimar Constitution, the Parliamentary Council sought to curb these instruments of popular will. Distrust of the masses was also made manifest in the limitation of the powers of the President, who under the Weimar Constitution had been the chief focus of plebiscitary democracy. Under previous German constitutions, the monarch or the Weimar President was regarded as the ultimate guardian of the constitution. The framers of the Basic Law were wary of giving executive power to the Federal President. They gave it instead to the Federal Constitutional Court.

Because of this looking backwards to Weimar, and because of this distrust, the Basic Law was, in the words of Carl Friedrich, the product of the negative revolutions of the post-war era, of a third force between revolution and counter-revolution which sought to find a sane *modus vivendi* between destructive extremes. In what way does the Basic Law exhibit this quality of negative revolution? The Basic Law is not so much the expression of forward-looking enthusiasm as one of deep revulsion towards a distasteful past. With its distrust of the common man, the attempt to reconstruct democracy without the *demos* could lead only to what German critics of the Basic Law have called the 'mediatization of the people' through political parties. The Basic Law started a stable governmental system in which the elite, namely the moderate parties, civil service and judges, ran the democratic show in West Germany until the people had a chance to learn democracy by experience. West Germany became a state which set out to establish stable democracy, but one based on the rule of the political classes. It was a state after the formula of men such as Schumpeter and Karl Mannheim. According to Mannheim, the fact that the shaping of policy is in the hands of elites does not mean that society is not democratic. It is sufficient, Mannheim believed, for democracy that the individual citizens, though prevented from taking a direct part in government all the time, have at least the *possibility* of making their aspirations felt.

There is, then, virtually no referendum any more in West Germany. The President is elected by the *Bundestag* and *Bundesrat,* not by the people. They can only vote for approved parties every 4 years. The President is a figurehead. He can neither appoint nor dismiss the Chancellor anymore. The Chancellor's position in the Basic Law is much stronger than that of the Weimar Constitution. In two recent studies, it was even suggested that the idea of a referendum on the formation of the separate Federal Republic of Germany and the idea of a constitution based on the sovereign will of the people were deliberately sacrificed because of the Cold War situation (see Niclauß 1992 and Jung 1992).

In respect of the continuation of the political classes, it has to be said that the civil service, responsible for the administration of the whole country, was not radically transformed, despite denazification. Very soon its personnel were very much the same as they had been during the Third Reich. It was not subjected to a process of democratization, either in terms of its structure – it retained its traditional hierarchy – or in terms of its attitude towards the state. This was excused with reference to necessity. General Lucius Clay wrote to

Eisenhower that the only people in West Germany who could be used in a rapid rebuilding of the administration were the old civil servants, all of whom had been members of the NSDAP, and the majority of these not just nominal members. So in the years of Allied occupation there were economically and administratively important Nazis who were not persecuted. In fact the whole idea of denazification largely failed (see Chapter 7).

A further point to be discussed is the decentralization of industry, and along with this the question of nationalization of industry – or, put in political terms, depriving the leading capitalists of their economic and political power. Up to the spring of 1948, the most powerful factor in post-war German economic life had been the labour movement, which enjoyed the active promotion of the British, and the confidence of the American and French occupation authorities. The conditions of economic scarcity, devastation, and the problem of the multitudes impoverished by expulsion had created a certain solidarity among the political parties on economic and social issues. This was reflected in the endorsement of large-scale socialization not only by the SPD and the KPD, but also by the CDU/CSU and the FDP. It was also expressed in the common conviction that the many people who had lost everything as a result of the war and its aftermath should be reimbursed from the holdings of those who had accumulated considerable assets over the years of crisis. Immediately after the war, American anti-trust experts in the Western zones set about decentralizing German industry. Coal and steel trusts in the Ruhr district were turned into dozens of small firms. The three giant German banks were divided up into nine banks. A significant document of the period was the 3 February 1947 CDU Ahlen resolution. It maintained that the capitalist system had failed the national and social aspirations of the German people, and that, following the political and economic collapse, fundamental reconstruction was the only possibility. The Ahlen resolution claimed further that the content and aim of such a social and economic construction could no longer be capitalist profit and striving for power, but only the welfare of the people.

As late as September 1949, the CDU Minister-President of North Rhine-Westfalia, Karl Arnold, said that Germany must not hesitate to nationalize industry to protect it against egotistical and power-hungry profiteers. The reorganization of property relations in the industries of the Ruhr, Arnold believed, had become an irrevocable social principle. But things had changed in the meantime: West Germany was on her way to becoming one of the most capitalist countries in the world. By spring 1948, the new economic director of the Bizonal Economic

Administration, Ludwig Erhard, counting on Marshall Plan aid, had already steered a course towards the large-scale reconstruction of the German economy. West Germany was to pull itself up by the bootstraps under conditions of free enterprise, with the utmost encouragement from governmental agencies.

In June of the same year, the military authorities of the three Western zones revalued the hopelessly inflated *Reichsmark,* introducing a new currency, the *deutschmark* (DM), with the appropriate measures in respect of banking and foreign debts. This reform had a magical effect on the supply of consumer goods and services, which up till then had been traded on the black market and withheld during the last months before 'Day X'. Yet it also wiped out the savings and cash holdings of large numbers of 'little people', while those in possession of merchandise, industrial capital, and other real assets got off to a head-start in the economic boom that followed. German authorities played only a subordinate, advisory role in this currency reform. The economic measures and the currency reform with its grave social and economic injustice immediately produced a general restoration of the old propertied classes to positions of power and influence. In June 1948, the journal of the British zone trade unions still noted with surprise and indignation the re-emergence of monopolists and erstwhile financers of Adolf Hitler.

Within 5 months, the trade unions felt compelled to organize a work stoppage involving more than 9 million workers. This dramatic event took place in defence of economic democracy. But after this demonstration of power, union strength gradually waned under the impact of mounting unemployment, rising prices and the prestige of economic success shared by the Adenauer administration and German business. The economic restoration brought with it the return of persons to influence who felt a great nostalgia for the good old days before 1939, 1933 or even 1914; and that meant both a strong-man government (Adenauer) and an authoritarian society (cf. Laitenberger 1988).

Although the worker had now got a certain modicum of political rights, there was still a considerable lack of *economic* rights. In this respect, things had not changed much since the nineteenth century. The trade unions did not seek to destroy capitalism: they wanted to rid Germany of monopolists because of the political threat they posed, to see some degree of nationalization introduced and, most of all, they wanted codetermination, both within the factories and in West German economic politics. One aim was that workers should make up half the board of directors in firms. The Allies promised codetermination in 1946, but, after 1949, a German law was required. In 1951 the trade unions threatened to strike. A compromise was finally reached between Adenauer and the trade unions: while the nationalization issue was sidestepped, there was to be codetermination in the coal, iron and steel industries, as well as in firms with more than 1000 employees. But nowhere else was it introduced.

This was the end of direct economic democracy in West Germany for the time being. In 1957, the SPD dropped nationalization from its agenda, although it still supported codetermination. The 1957 SPD Bad Godesberg Programme stated that the Social Democratic Party had changed from a party of the working classes to a party of the people.

DEVELOPMENTS IN THE SOVIET ZONE

The GDR and the FRG, both founded in 1949, were the product of the Second World War and the ever-increasing rift between East and West. To some extent, political, economic and societal developments in the Soviet zone between 1945 and 1949 not only were congruent with the Potsdam Agreements, but also in fact constituted a proper implementation of them (cf. Janßen 1996). Nowadays it is generally accepted that neither the Soviet Union nor political leaders in the Soviet zone were interested in a separate state in the immediate post-war years. It is more likely that there was a genuine belief in the Soviet zone that a new society could be created which would look attractive to the working classes throughout the zones. Within such a framework, developments in the Soviet zone become more comprehensible, for a number of these developments were not only congruent with the Potsdam Agreements, but also laid the foundations for the establishment of a Marxist-Leninist state in the GDR. These so-called 'anti-fascist democratic' measures also in some instances met the aspirations of political leaders and the populace at large.

Developments in the Soviet zone were rapid, at times breathtakingly so. On 30 April 1945, the day Hitler committed suicide, a group of ten Germans known as the 'Ulbricht Group' landed at Frankfurt/Oder airport. Another group of Germans, the 'Ackermann Group', soon followed. Both groups were led by established communist leaders, Walter Ulbricht and Anton Ackermann, but consisted of predominantly non-communist anti-fascists. The remit of these groups was to assist the Soviet Military Administration (SMA) in its task of running the Soviet zone. The SMA encouraged the development of political and trade-union life. The Communist Party published its

manifesto on 11 June 1945, just over a month after Germany's surrender, and before the Potsdam Conference. The Social Democrats
followed suit within a matter of days. The Christian Democrats issued
their proclamation on 26 June, followed by the Liberals.

Neither the spectrum of parties nor their programmes differed from
those which emerged in the Western zones. Even the concept of close
inter-party cooperation following the total collapse of Germany and
its consequences was a popular one in all zones. In the Soviet zone,
however, it assumed a much more stringent form on 14 July 1945, with
the establishment of the 'United Front of Anti-Fascist and Democratic
Parties' at state, district, municipal and local level. The United Front
was a fundamental strategic device of the Leninist party, but it was
nevertheless welcomed by the non-communist parties and the trade
union movement (in the Western zones, however, *Antifa* committees
were forbidden after their emergence). In the block committees which
were formed at all levels, all parties had equal representation and the
right of veto. However, with the formation of the Socialist Unity Party
(SED) in April 1946, the situation began to change considerably. The
fusion of Social Democrats and Communists reflected the sentiments
of many working-class people who had experienced the split of the
labour movement in 1917, and who saw labour disunity as one of the
factors in Hitler's rise to power. But the manner of the fusion met with
disapproval, not only from the Western Social Democrat leaders, but
also from members in the Soviet zone. The formation of the SED
resulted in a shift of emphasis within the United Front, for the SED
proclaimed itself in favour of a socialist society beyond an anti-fascist
democratic order. Furthermore, the trade union movement was incor-
porated into the United Front, as were other new parties which were
de facto communist-led, such as the National Democrats (NDPD) and
the Democratic Farmer's Party (DBD).

Party-political developments were underpinned by revolutionary
changes in society and the economy. A major event was the land
reform of September 1945, a programme initiated by all parties in
Saxony, although two leading Christian Democrats would not agree
to the expropriation of the landed gentry without compensation. A
further major reconstruction of the economy started with the large-
scale expropriation of industries in October 1945, which began in
Saxony and was overwhelmingly supported by the population in a
plebiscite. In June 1948, there followed the adoption of a centrally
planned economy. By now the course was truly set for a Marxist-
Leninist state. In the course of the implementation of the Potsdam
agreements, changes in the Soviet zone had followed the letter of the

then current handbook of socialist political economy (Akademie der Wissenschaften 1955: 664f.). On the other hand, the fact that the British had plans for land reform, industrial reorganization and a planned economy seems to contradict the notion that developments in the Soviet zone must of necessity be classified as a socialist-Stalinist revolution.

The formation of the United Front in the summer of 1947 did not prevent individual parties from standing for local elections on separate platforms. Until October 1946, a multi-party situation prevailed in elections within the five *Länder* of the Soviet zone. Despite the fact that some parties were inhibited in their election campaigns, the *Länder* elections of 20 October 1946 indicated the relative strengths of the individual parties, with the SED narrowly missing an absolute majority in three of the states, i.e. Mecklenburg, Thuringia and Saxony. A further interesting feature of these elections was the participation of two mass organizations, the Farmers' Mutual Aid Association (VdgB), and the League of Culture for the Democratic Renewal of Germany. The VdgB had been formed in the wake of the land reform to provide technical and financial aid and advice for the newly created farms. Organizationally, its leadership was in the hands of the SED. The League of Culture was founded on the initiative of the SMA in July 1945 as part of the democratization process in Germany, with the object of eliminating fascism in the cultural sphere. Both the VdgB and the League of Culture, along with the trade union movement and the Free German Youth, became part of the United Front. Within the remit of the anti-fascist bloc, and in the historical context of the fight against the remnants of fascism and the creation of a new Germany, such an inclusion of the mass organizations made sense. But in the context of party political tradition this phenomenon constituted a radical innovation and a contrast to developments in the Western zones. It was to prove an important initiative for the organization of political life in the German Democratic Republic.

The People's Congress Movement is of prime importance for an understanding of constitutional and political life in the GDR. To counteract separatist developments in the Western zones, and in anticipation of the London Conference of Foreign Ministers in November and December 1947, the leadership of the SED called on all political parties, trade unions, and other mass organizations to form an all-German 'People's Congress Movement for Unity and a Just Peace' in order that the threat of a permanently divided Germany might be averted. The SED attempted to place itself at the head of a movement with a potentially wide appeal throughout Germany. The first congress was timed to coincide with the London Conference, and took place on 6–7 December 1947 in Berlin. It was attended by 2215 delegates, of whom 664 came from the Western zones. The second congress convened on 18 March 1948, the anniversary of the 1848 bourgeois-democratic revolution with its aim of a new unified Germany. The second congress elected a People's Council of 400 members to act as an all-German representative assembly.

In the meantime, the People's Congress Movement had been outlawed in the Western zones. The second congress also established six committees, one of which, under Otto Grotewohl, was to work out a constitution for an all-German Democratic Republic. The Congress Movement also initiated a signature campaign in May/June 1948 calling for a plebiscite on the question of German unity. 14 million signatures were gathered, representing 37 per cent of the German electorate. In March 1949, the People's Council decided to hold a third congress. This was at a time when West Berlin was subject to the Berlin Blockade (see Chapter 3) and preparations for a West German constitution were well under way. Elections for this third congress were planned for May 1949, and were to take place on the basis of so-called 'unified lists' whereby candidates were nominated by the individual parties and mass organizations, and the total membership of the People's Council was distributed according to a predetermined key. The SED was to be allocated 25 per cent of the seats, the CDU and LDPD (Liberal Democrats) 15 per cent each, the NDPD and the DBD 7.5 per cent each, the Free German Trade Unions 10 per cent, the Free German Youth Movement and the League of Culture 5 per cent each. The rest was to go to other mass organizations. On 15 and 16 May 1949, elections were held on the basis of a 'yes' or 'no' vote for the lists and aims of congress: 61.8 per cent of the population in the Soviet zone, and 51.7 per cent of the population of the Soviet sector in Berlin voted 'yes'. The third congress on 30 May 1949 accepted the proposed constitution for a German Democratic Republic. On 7 October 1949, this constitution became the constitution of the newly formed GDR, and the second People's Council became the parliament or People's Chamber. The first elections for the People's Chamber took place on 15 October 1950, again using the system of a unified list with seats distributed according to a predetermined key. The People's Congress Movement was renamed the National Front of a Democratic Germany. The principles of unified list and predetermined distribution, finalized in 1963, remained in force until 1989.

THE SED, THE CONSTITUTION AND THE STATE

The key allotted 127 members to the SED, 52 each to the LDPD, CDU, NDPD, and DBD, 68 members to the trade union movement, 40 to the Free German Youth movement, 35 to the Democratic Women's League, and 22 to the League of Culture. These principles were by no means uncontested, and at the least constituted bargaining points between the SED and the other parties. Naturally the other parties were aware that the mass organizations were either led by SED members, dependent on the SED, or indeed had already declared themselves as comrades-in-arms of the SED. Furthermore, developments had taken place which had changed the party political scene substantially. Party formation had merely been a first stage in this shift. The formation of the DBD and the NDPD had been initiated under the auspices of the SED, and both the new parties declared themselves to be its partners. Significantly, they were a departure from the existing party framework, inasmuch as they were conceived as interest groups. The DBD was to mobilize and enlist the support of the farmers, the NDPD that of the middle classes, including the small entrepreneurs, former professional soldiers, and ex-Nazis. In the meantime, the SED had declared itself a party of the new type in January 1949, i.e. it had become a Marxist-Leninist party.

Given these developments, the new constitution of 7 October 1949 was already at variance with political reality. In the economy, developments were moving rapidly towards a socialist mode of production, and in party politics the primacy of the SED had already been established. The 1949 constitution was closely modelled on the Weimar constitution, and the word 'socialism' was nowhere to be found. This can of course be easily explained by the history of the constitution, which was after all intended to serve the whole of Germany. During the 18 years of its life, the gap between the letter of the constitution and political practice widened considerably, due partly to internal and partly to external developments. Finally, in 1967, on the occasion of the 7th Party Congress of the SED, Walter Ulbricht announced that a new constitution would be drafted, and this was duly implemented by the setting up of a constitutional committee of the People's Chamber. The new constitution of 1968 referred to itself as 'socialist'; the primacy of the SED was laid down constitutionally; all power was to be exercised by the working people; compared with 1949, the new constitution omitted a number of inviolable basic rights, such as the right to strike; the concept of an indivisible Germany no longer featured, instead the GDR defined itself as a 'socialist state of the

German nation'. This phrase was amended in the 1974 version where the reference to 'the German nation' was eliminated. Whereas the 1968 constitution did not refer to 'communism', this was changed by the 1974 amendments. Finally, the 1974 amendments strengthened constitutionally the bond with the Soviet Union.

It is extremely problematic to apply Western concepts of the state and constitutional concepts such as the division of powers to the GDR. It is more appropriate to ask: Who was responsible to whom? What were the functions of the People's Chamber? Who introduced bills? What was the role of the parties? Who had executive powers? Who elected whom?

According to Article 48 of the constitution, the People's Chamber was the embodiment of the principle of the people's sovereignty, and it was the highest organ of power. The people exercised their sovereignty through the election of the 500 members every 5 years. The members of the People's Chamber were not professional politicians; they were otherwise gainfully employed, and merely received attendance allowances and a free rail card. According to GDR statistics, between 1981 and 1986 47.2 per cent of the members were workers, 10.4 per cent were farmers, farm workers, etc., 17.8 per cent were public service employees and 23 per cent were members of the intelligentsia. 32.4 per cent were women. Members were organized in groups either according to their party or mass organization. Each group had the right to put questions and motions, and to make statements. Additionally, each group could initiate laws, a right also held by the Council of Group Leaders, any 15 members, and the leadership of the trade union movement. However, this right was only ever exercised by the Council of Ministers and the Council of State. The Council of Group Leaders was responsible for the proper running of the Chamber according to standing orders. The actual participation in the decision-making processes took place in 15 committees dealing among other things with foreign affairs, defence, industry, housing and transportation. Each committee worked according to an annual plan, and had a right to information and control. The Council of Ministers was obliged to inform committees about governmental action, and had to consider the conclusions arrived at in the work of the committees. Committees could demand that the minister be present during their deliberations. One of the committees' major tasks was to deliberate on bills and to discuss these with the public.

Plenary sessions of the People's Chamber steadily decreased; between 1976 and 1981, the chamber met only 13 times in plenary session. The People's Chamber decided on fundamental questions of government policy, and combined legislative and executive powers. Its executive organs were the Council of State, the Council of Ministers, the National Council for Defence, and the highest organs of the judiciary. The fundamental decisions of the People's Council formed the basis of the activities of the state apparatus. The overwhelming majority of these decisions were taken unanimously. The People's Chamber also appointed the Council of State and its Chair, the Chair of the Council of Ministers and, on his or her nominations, the ministers, the Chair of the National Council for Defence, the President and judges of the High Court and the Chief Public Prosecutor.

Elections were in the hands of the National Front of the GDR. Parties and mass organizations suggested candidates' names, which were placed on the unified list, ultimately decided on by the SED. Candidates were then presented to the public at meetings organized by the National Front. At this stage the electorate could propose the rejection of a candidate; however, the final decision rested with the National Front. The same procedure applied at district and regional (county) level. The actual elections were mere acts of approbation, although it was possible to score out the name of a candidate; but it would have required more than 50 per cent of the electorate to do so to stop a candidate from being elected.

Neither the elections nor the numerical allocation of seats revealed anything about the actual decision-making power. It is interesting to note, for instance, that out of the 68 trade union members in the last People's Chamber, 61 were also enrolled members of the SED, while the vast majority of the members from the Free German Youth Movement, the Democratic Women's League and the League of Culture were also SED members and thus bound by the SED party statute. Two hundred and eighty-one SED members in the People's Chamber were subject to party discipline, so that a majority of members of parliament was accountable to the SED. The same, of course, applied to regional and district councils, and, most importantly, at National Front level. Furthermore, the constitution itself established the primacy of the working class and its Marxist-Leninist party. Close cooperation and personal overlap also existed between the state apparatus, the apparatus of the mass organizations and the SED party organization.

There was therefore a high concentration of power within the SED. Concomitantly, the state apparatus followed the SED's lead as the executive arm of the party's policies. The SED was not just a party within the state, the state itself was part of the party. According to the constitution, the multi-party system had as its aim the integration of the dynamics of the people. The other four parties thereby became channels of communication and mobilization, fulfilling Lenin's concept of the transmission belt. The multi-party system also shifted the burden of responsibility away from the SED, not only internally, where the SED could utilize the DBP in the farm collectivization programme, but also externally when, for example, members of the CDU acted as unofficial ambassadors for the GDR. Nevertheless, possibly because of the political if not organizational dependence on the SED, the membership of the four other parties declined after 1949.

The SED, according to its party statute, was structured on and functioned according to the principle of democratic centralism. Among other things this meant that the politburo was the chief policy-making body in the GDR. The structure of the SED showed a clear congruence with the state apparatus along governmental and administrative lines. This was consolidated by personnel overlap between the state and party apparatus. Members of the politburo and the Central Committee Secretariat were also often members of the Council of State, the Council of Ministers and Chairs of the committees of the People's Chamber. In terms of decision-making, the system of government was characterized predominantly by the issuing of directives which originated in the higher echelons of the party hierarchy and proceeded via party congresses to the apparatus of state such as the People's Chamber.

3 The two German states
Realities and images

THE QUESTION OF RESPONSIBILITY

The proclamation of two constitutions and different state concepts in 1949 confirmed the division of Germany between the two Cold War power blocs. The 1950s saw a gradual further integration of West Germany into the Western bloc, and East Germany into the Eastern bloc as the Cold War between the former Allies was stepped up. It was in September 1950 that the USA first seriously proposed the rearmament of West Germany at a meeting of NATO foreign ministers in New York; less than 5 years later, in 8 May 1955, West Germany formally became a member of both the Western European Union (WEU) and NATO. One year after this, on 21 July 1956, legislation was approved in Bonn introducing conscription. Military integration was flanked by economic and political integration. In April 1951, West Germany and five other Western states established the European Coal and Steel Community (ECSC); in May of the same year, the Council of Europe accepted the Federal Republic as a full member. In March 1957, West Germany and the five other ECSC members signed the Treaty of Rome – thereby establishing the European Economic Community (EEC) and the European Atomic Energy Community (EUROTOM). As the West's grip on West Germany tightened, so did the East's on East Germany – often in response. Nine days after West Germany's entry into NATO, on 14 May 1955, the Warsaw Pact was signed, with East Germany a co-signatory. It was also in May 1955 that the GDR signed 20-year treaties of friendship, cooperation and mutual assistance with other Eastern bloc countries. In September 1955, East German sovereignty was formally restored. As West Germany developed along the lines of Western European democracy based on federal structures, East Germany in the 1950s – with some vacillation – developed into a centralist socialist state. Within 10 years of the war, the two countries were already so different and not just divided, but allied to new constellations to which they would remain attached until the late 1980s.

But who was responsible for this process of division? Historical evidence suggests that the Soviet Union was not interested in a division of Germany in the immediate post-war years. Stalin maintained on 9 May 1945 that, although the Soviet Union was celebrating its victory, it did not intend to carve up Germany. Even a staunchly anti-communist historian such as Golo Mann conceded that the partition of Germany was not in the interest of the latter [i.e. the Soviets] because they firmly controlled their own zone anyway. Influence over the rest, particularly the Ruhr (in which they were especially interested) they could only gain if Germany remained united. Had they wanted or foreseen the division of Germany they would never have agreed to make Berlin the seat of the four occupying powers (Mann 1974: 817f).

By contrast, the French were strongly committed to the fragmentation of Germany. On 14 September 1945, they submitted a document to the Conference at Potsdam in which a partitioning was advocated. This stance was reiterated at the Paris Session of the Council of Foreign Ministers (between 25 April and 15 May 1946). According to Alfred Grosser, a French historian, France was largely responsible for the fact that an 'Austrian' solution could not be found for Germany (Grosser 1974: 103).

Less well propagated than the Soviet and French attitudes are those of the British, Americans and those Germans who were to shape the course of post-war West German history, such as Konrad Adenauer. It is noteworthy that the Americans changed course (i.e. concerning German unity) as early as the Potsdam Conference at which they proposed that the Soviet zone should be Russia's reparation territory, while the Western Allies would help themselves from their zones and hand over only 10 percent to the East. This solution in practice meant abandoning the economic unity of Germany which the victors had wanted to preserve (Mann 1974: 819).

This American solution is unlikely to have been put forward in order to find a workable reparations administration. In early summer 1945, before the Potsdam Conference, the American expert on Soviet Russian affairs, George F. Kennan, suggested that it was nonsense to imagine that Germany could be governed jointly, or that the Soviets and Americans could simply withdraw from Germany one day. Kennan saw no alternative to establishing a strong, independent, separate West Germany. He admitted that this would mean dismembering

Germany; whether the Soviet zone would eventually be united with the rest was not important to him. Kennan preferred a divided Germany, with her Western part acting as a buffer between the Western and Eastern blocs, to a united Germany which might make possible the spreading of Communist influence westwards.

Kennan saw the Americans and the Soviets as inevitable rivals in Germany, and therefore suggested that no concessions be made to the Soviets in the Control Commission. The same ideas were harboured by a man who for almost 2 decades was to be the most influential politician in West Germany, namely Konrad Adenauer. As early as October 1945, Adenauer declared in an interview with the *News Chronicle* and *Associated Press* that the Western Allies should form a Federal Republic on the basis of their zones. In order to pacify France and Belgium, Adenauer suggested the economic integration of West Germany, France and Belgium. He eventually had his way within his own party, the CDU, against strong opposition, and the Americans could thus rely on a good friend for their separatist plans. The implementation of these ideas was made easier by the anti-communist attitudes displayed by Kurt Schumacher, who bluntly refused to have anything to do with the East German SED, which was one of the reasons why Jakob Kaiser's (CDU) initiatives for an all-party stance on German unity were wrecked. All this happened, moreover, in a climate in which West Germans were not very interested in unity. Even in 1951, 'when the West German Institute of Public Opinion asked people what they thought was the most important question facing Germany, only 18 per cent replied reunification, compared with 45 per cent who replied that it was the economic conditions' (Cecil 1971: 2f.).

It did not take long to put these separatist ideas into practice. Plans for the establishment of West Germany emerged, and were sanctioned by the Western Allies long before 1949, without the Germans or indeed the Soviets having any say in the matter (cf. Steininger 1983). Although bizonal agreements of various kinds between the British and Americans had already been made, the speech by American Secretary of State, J. F. Byrnes, at Stuttgart in September 1946, is generally seen as the turning-point in post-war German history. Byrnes said:

> We favour the economic unification of Germany. If complete unification cannot be secured, we shall do everything in our power to secure maximum possible unification. [...] It [i.e. the American Government] has formally announced that its intention is to unify the economy of its own zone with any or all of the other

zones willing to participate in the unification. So far, only the British Government has agreed to let its zone participate.

(Ruhm von Oppen 1955: 155)

This policy resulted in the economic agreement between the British and Americans in December 1946, to which the French acceded in November 1947 after the declaration of the Truman doctrine and the announcement of the Marshall Aid Plan. The British and Americans blandly reiterated their claim that such a fusion would be economic only, not political. In February 1947, the British Military Governor Sir Sholto Douglas stated that 'no agreement whatever exists for the political fusion of the British and American zones; nor have any plans for this end been discussed' (Ruhm von Oppen 1955: 218).

Yet on 7 November 1947, Averell Harriman, who was responsible for trade in the Washington administration, sent a report to President Truman advocating some form of German government, as this would be absolutely necessary for a revitalization of the economy. Harriman found that the formation of a government encompassing all four zones was no longer desirable nor possible; therefore the Western Allies must start with what they had got. This point of view was underlined by a report made by Lewis H. Brown, Chairman of the Board of Johns-Manville Corporation, to General Lucius D. Clay in July 1947, in which a total integration of the Western zones was seen as necessary. On 20 October 1947, the US State Department stated that Germany had become a divided country. The communiqué issued by the London Six-Power Conference on 7 June 1948 confirmed the emergence of West Germany as a separate state.

In this context, Stalin's blockade of Berlin between June 1948 and May 1949 must be read as a desperate attempt to prevent the currency reform in the Western zone and thus the economic and political division of Germany. According to Allied agreement Berlin was to be jointly administered, but the initially disguised introduction of the new Western deutschmark into Berlin indicated a policy of brinkmanship. In fact, the introduction of the new deutschmark in the Western zones in itself constituted a clear violation of the Potsdam accord, but according to the slogan 'whoever controls the currency wields the power' (first propagated by the Berlin SPD leader Ernst Reuter), the currency reform was a power-political measure. Stalin attempted to counteract it by stopping the exchange of goods between the two halves of the city, and blockading all access by land and water to Western Berlin. The Western response was a spectacular airlift without historical parallel. West Berlin's population of 2.5 million was supplied by 270,000 flights during the 262 days of the blockade.

At no point during these years was there any instance where the German people were given a say on the issue of separation through elections. It has been argued that a deliberate policy decision by the Western Allies prevented the German population from voting on this issue (Woods Eisenberg 1996). An example from the Paris Peace Conference in May 1949 illustrates how set the Western Allies were on the partition of Germany. Stalin had made proposals to reverse the partitioning process. The Western powers countered with a demand that there should be an Allied High Commission where decisions be taken by majority vote, and the right of veto abolished – which would have been totally unacceptable to the Soviets. Nevertheless, the Americans were worried that Stalin might accept this proposal. General Lucius D. Clay wrote in his memoirs: 'It would have been the end of our efforts to form a West German government.' He stated that he was glad when the Soviets finally turned down the proposal (Steele 1977: 70f). The German people in the Western zones no more than rubber-stamped developments when they went to the ballot boxes for the election of the West German *Bundestag* and ratification of the Basic Law in August 1949. On the other hand, the Western Allies had all the time paid lip-service to the German 'national will'. The British Deputy Military Governor, Sir Brian Robertson, said in October 1946:

> It is clear that a final answer to the future structure of Germany cannot be given until the country is united, until full agreement on the matter has been reached between the Allies and until the German people themselves are able to express their national will.
> (Ruhm von Oppen 1955: 188)

Despite Western propaganda duplicity towards German 'self-determination' until 1949, it was to become one of the major arguments in the West used against the German Democratic Republic. In February 1950, the High Commissioner of the USA, John J. McCloy, declared at a press conference that the political unification of Germany on the basis of free elections was one of the major aims of his country's foreign policy. Yet the three Western powers declared on 19 September 1950 that they considered 'the Government of the Federal Republic as the only German Government freely and legitimately constituted and therefore entitled to speak for Germany as the representative of the German people in international affairs' (Ruhm von Oppen 1955: 517). Not content with stating a legalistic case, the

West began to pursue a 'policy of strength' towards the GDR and the Soviet Union, which determined the relationship between the two German states until 1968. As early as March 1952, Chancellor Adenauer declared that, once the Soviets found themselves confronted by a rearmed West Germany, they would be happy to negotiate. Adenauer, together with John F. Dulles, who became American Secretary of State in 1953, embarked on a policy of containment, roll-back, or, to put it more bluntly, military brinkmanship. In that same March of 1952, Stalin suggested all-German free elections and a peace-treaty on the lines of the Austrian solution, i.e. neutrality for Germany. The three Western powers turned this proposal down flat, arguing that a united Germany should be free to enter any treaty with whomsoever it desired (see Steininger 1983: Vol. 2, Chap. 16).

Adenauer's own response to Stalin's peace treaty proposals was delivered to the parliamentary executive committee of the CDU/ CSU on 25 March. It demonstrated not only his commitment to the Western 'policy of strength' but, even more importantly, his lack of interest at the time in negotiations on the question of German unity. He believed rather in building up Western military might as an 'argument' for the future. His argument was that, when the reconstruction of Europe happened, as he believed it would, then this would also entail the reconstruction of eastern Europe. It would be important to talk to the Soviets at the right moment, and that would only be possible in a scenario where the West was strong, forcing the Soviets to listen. But such a moment could not be envisaged for the immediate future, and negotiations with the Soviets at the present moment would be positively detrimental to Western interests (Bodensieck 1972: 52f.). Members of the SPD opposition adopted similar attitudes of aggression, proclaiming that the Federal Republic was identical with the German *Reich* of 1937. Parliamentarian Adolf Arndt exclaimed on 4 December 1952 in the *Bundestag* that the Federal Republic also embraced Saarbrücken, Greater Berlin, Dresden, Breslau [Wroclaw] and Königsberg [Kaliningrad] (Bodensieck 1972: 52f.).

While negotiations were taking place between the Federal Republic and the Western powers on the Paris Treaties, which were to re-arm West Germany and integrate it into NATO, the Soviet foreign minister, Molotov, attempted once more to open negotiations on the question of German unity with a proposal dated 1 February 1954. One has to bear in mind that at this time the final settlement concerning Austria was being negotiated, which made Austria a neutral sovereign country in May 1955. Molotov proposed free all-German elections for 1955. But Adenauer and the Western powers chose not to take up

Molotov's offer. Adenauer declared that one could deal with the Soviet proposals just as well after the ratification of the Paris Treaties, which of course were to seal the final division of Germany. He told Ollenhauer, the leader of the SPD, which was against the Treaties, that he was prepared to negotiate on everything which the Soviet Union had said about the German question in the last days and weeks – either before or after ratification (Bodensieck 1972: 60). In retrospect, this seems an almost cynical statement, especially since it is now clear that these Soviet proposals of 1954 arguably marked the last chance for a united Germany. The Western opposition to a united Germany was also demonstrated by Harold Macmillan, who remarked in the House of Commons in 1955: 'If Germany is to be neutral and armed, who is to keep her neutral? If she is to be neutral and disarmed, who is to keep her disarmed?' (Cecil 1971: 20). On 5 May 1955, the three Western powers and the Federal Republic declared that they had one aim: a united Germany with a constitution similar to that of the Federal Republic and integrated into the European community. Neither the Soviet Union nor the GDR could be expected to agree to this.

On at least three occasions, then, all-German elections could have been possible, but the Western powers, including Adenauer's government, rejected them as inopportune. Instead, they pursued an aggressive policy of partition and opposed the possibility of a neutral united Germany – a policy of strength which proved to be totally misguided, given that the Soviet Union gained increasingly in military might. Calls for 'free elections' and 'self-determination' were little more than ideological slogans which did not reflect actual Western policies. These facts of division do not tally with a popular belief among West Germans that division was due to the conflict between the Soviet Union and the Western powers, or indeed solely to the aggression of the Soviets. What people came to believe was the result of Cold War propaganda.

DISCOURSE OF A DIVIDED GERMANY

What mattered in this ideological propaganda war between West and East was not so much the facts as how these were represented. Distorted images of reality were a key feature of this discourse, images which apportioned blame for division and, implicitly, served as a means of self-exculpation. The Western propaganda of inculpation was highly successful and helped by the fact that, from the moment

of the formation of the SED, the GDR proved to be an odious dictatorship. Not only did the FRG turn out to be more successful economically, its political system was more acceptable to its citizens. No-
one can claim that what passed for socialism in the GDR was started
under favourable conditions, or implemented democratically. East
Germans, after having been abandoned by the West, had to learn to
live with the GDR, even if the majority never learnt to love it. But they
also had to learn to live with the fact that, despite their economic
success within the Eastern bloc context, they were ignored or even
disparaged for their efforts. For decades, the 'golden West' dubbed
them 'our poor brothers and sisters in the East'. Adenauer's refusal to
recognize East Germany, underpinned as of 1955 by the Hallstein
Doctrine in accordance with which the FRG threatened to break off
diplomatic relations with states which recognized the GDR, was
designed to undermine the legitimacy of the GDR and therefore its
right to represent German interests. From the beginning, the GDR
was a 'bastard' state in Western propaganda. East Germans felt not
just that they were being blamed for division, or for the odium of
dictatorship, but that their lives were somehow tarred with the brush
of illegitimacy.

   Even after the advent of *ostpolitik* (see Chapter Four), this attitude of
inculpation was noticeable. In 1978, a paperback appeared in the
Federal Republic comprising extracts from over two thousand essays
on the subject of unification written by West German school children
and apprentices between the ages of 14 and 24, i.e. a generation of
young people who were born at least 1 to 2 decades after the war at
the inception and zenith of the West German economic miracle
(Boßmann 1978). What had this new generation come to believe?
The youngsters blamed the GDR and her ally the Soviet Union for
everything; the West was always looking for unification, the GDR
always obstructing it. West German official government publications
did much to inculcate this attitude. Thus it was claimed that West
Germany had come about as the unavoidable response to Soviet
attempts to block political progress (cf. Press and Information Office
1972: 55f). Even one of the most recent German government publications of 1994 stated unequivocally that it was Stalin's brutal actions in
the Eastern bloc which increased conflicts with the Western powers,
and that the currency reform in the Western zones was an opportunity
'seized' by Stalin to withdraw from the Allied Control Council and the
commandatura in Berlin (Presse- und Informationsamt 1994: 11).
Moreover, West Germany was presented as a bulwark against the
continued threat of Soviet imperialism. One school text book claimed

that the Soviet Union sought not only to exploit its zone for its own benefit, but, at an opportune moment, to extend its influence over the whole of Germany (Thurich and Endlich 1971: 12).

In this tradition of West German inculpation, certain dates and events took on a highly symbolic significance, serving as propaganda icons. Thus the Berlin blockade came to symbolize Western commitment to freedom on the one hand, and Eastern repression and power politics on the other. Constantly evoking this blockade in subsequent decades served to keep the contrastive view of West and East in public consciousness. The 17 June 1953 uprising in the GDR also became loaded with symbolic value. When workers involved in the building of East Berlin's showpiece *Stalinallee* took to the streets to demand more freedom and better working conditions, they were soon joined by thousands all over East Germany. The brutal suppression by Soviet tanks is historical fact. However, when the Federal Republic declared 17 June a day of national unity, a ritualized and tendentious act of commemoration set in. The 17 June 1953 did illustrate that the East German regime had to rely on Soviet tanks to continue its existence; but it had not originally or even ultimately been a demonstration for a unified Germany. Until 1990, FRG commemoration of the 17 June was little more than a reiterated political statement to the effect that the Soviets had prevented democracy and unification.

The Berlin Wall, built in August 1961 by the GDR, incarcerated a whole people. It demonstrated the powerlessness of the East German regime to deal with the attraction of the 'golden West', and the failure to project the GDR as the state of workers and farmers. There is no doubt that it was the Soviet Union and East Germany which, literally, reinforced the division the West had so avidly accelerated in the 1950s. But there was a tendency in the West to equate the GDR with the fences, walls, mines and shootings at the German–German border. This tendency continued after 1990, when the quite legitimate trials of borderguards were given a media and political prominence that reflected this tradition of West German reductionism. The presence of the Wall did appear to confirm Western views of the East as repressive. More often than not, however, the Wall became a point of reference justifying tough, indeed excessive West German measures against communists and communist sympathizers in the FRG.

By contrast, West Germany presented *itself* as being economically and democratically superior. The West German economic miracle *(Wirtschaftswunder)* was the most powerful of these self-congratulatory projections. It was an idealization. West Germany inherited much modern industrial plant from the Third Reich's war economy, plant which had been operated by forced labour from 1942 to 1945 and frequently left unscathed by Allied bombing. Not only, then, was the miracle not so miraculous, its preconditions were morally questionable. The image of a successful West German democracy and a dynamic economy resulted in the self-projected concept of *Modell Deutschland,* a model to be followed by others. The validity of this model has, from time to time, been doubted in the light of such issues as poverty, the integration problems experienced by foreign guest-workers and their families, democracy deficits and environmental problems. The image of *Modell Deutschland* remained intact, however, even at the time of the greatest democracy crisis in West Germany in 1968 when the German student movement threatened the very basis of the state, and certainly its education system.

East Germany also had its own inculpatory propaganda images. Indeed one might talk of 'counter-icons'. Thus in the GDR the 17 June 1953 uprising came to represent the interference of the Americans, whose intelligence organizations were accused of attempting a coup, in the GDR's internal affairs. The Berlin Wall was sold to the East German populace as self-protection against Western espionage and infiltration. But because such interpretations were patently absurd, they were not accepted by the broad masses. More effective was the GDR's long-standing attempt to present the FRG as what it called a 're-fascistized state'. If the West accused the East of repression, the East accused the West of rehabilitating those once guilty of repression and of drifting towards a capitalist dictatorship. While this case was more than a little overstated, it was lent credence by the GDR's success in uncovering Nazis living and working in the West – often in high office. Thus Hans Krüger, CDU Minister for Expellees, was forced to resign in January 1964 after the East Germans were able to prove that he had acted as judge at a court which had passed death sentences in Poland during the war. By contrast, East Germany presented itself as truly liberated from National Socialism (for more on coming to terms with the past, see Chapter 7).

Nowhere was the agenda of self-exculpation and inculpation in both East and West more conspicuous than in yearly acts of commemoration marking the end of the war (8 May 1945). In East Germany, the day was one of celebration. The Soviets were celebrated for having liberated Germany. But at the same time official statements emphasized that German socialists had played a role in liberating eastern Germany, and in helping to build up 'anti-fascist' structures after the war. 8 May thus also represented a self-liberation, making questions of responsibility for Nazism superfluous. Over the years, regular commemorations at the Berlin-Treptow Memorial to Soviet soldiers perversely implied that East Germans and Soviets had somehow been brothers in combat. The shoulder-to-shoulder retracing in 1985 of the path of the Red Army from the Oder to Berlin, enacted by Lenin Pioniers from the Soviet Union and East German Thälmann Pioneers, suggested that East Germans had been accompanying the Red Army in spirit if not in flesh. Such acts embedded 8 May within the continuing anti-fascist struggle. The essential inculpatory message was that the GDR and the Soviets had joined forces to resist the continued influence of fascism in the form of restorative West German capitalism and American imperialism. This argument placed the East Germans on the right side of the moral divide.

In West Germany, 8 May was initially thought of as the day of the 'military and political collapse of National Socialism', as the 5 May 1955 Federal government declaration put it. West German politicians referred to it as a day of sadness, grief, reflection, or as a watershed, a new beginning, the start of democracy. Not until Richard von Weizsäcker's famous speech in 1985 did 8 May enter public consciousness as a day of shame and guilt at Nazi atrocities. While gratitude towards the Americans, British and French was expressed in official speeches, it was usually gratitude for the post-war contribution to rebuilding West Germany. In the 1960s and 1970s, the term 'day of liberation' was rarely used in official parlance, indeed it was specifically rejected (for instance by Erhard in his radio address to the nation on 7 May 1965). The term was, of course, occupied by the GDR; by refusing to use it, West German politicians were able to throw into relief what they perceived to be the continuity of repression (Hitlerism replaced by Stalinism) and undermine the GDR's official rhetoric. Moreover, by expressing the view that liberation would be achieved only when Germany was once more democratically united, West German politicians projected blame for division on to the East, instrumentalizing commemorations in the interests of Cold War propaganda.

4 The intervening years
Long-term factors in change

THE IMPACT OF THE BERLIN WALL

One of the fundamental problems for the GDR was that it was not only not recognized by the FRG, but also not recognized by many of its own citizens. Between 1945 and 1961, 3,129,970 people left the Soviet zone and the GDR for West Germany. The forced pace of industrialization in the 1950s, the lack of consumer goods, the subjection of farmers to the collectivization programme, the discrimination of small businesses, as well as political and cultural repression generated considerable dissatisfaction hardly mitigated by the regime's rhetorical emphasis on the importance of labour or by the various 'perks' available to the workers such as free leisure activities. After the suppression of the 17 June 1953 uprising, and following the death of Stalin and the Kremlin-inspired introduction of the 'New Course' in the GDR, the GDR did benefit to a degree from the 'post-Stalinist' thaw, but by the late 1950s priorities had shifted again within the framework of a second 5-year plan (1956–1960) to the build-up of heavy industry at the expense of wage-earning consumers. Independent farmers came under renewed pressure to turn over their properties to collective farms. As of 1954 in the case of the Churches, and of 1956 in the case of political opposition, Ulbricht adopted an increasingly hard line. While the GDR made economic progress – industrial and handicraft production rose from 43.7 per cent of total output in 1950 to 53 per cent by 1960 – it was clear to East Germans that the West of the country offered greater wealth, freedom, more consumer goods and wages with greater purchasing power. When Khrushchev issued an ultimatum on 27 November 1958 insisting that, if the Western Allies did not leave West Berlin and agree to its status as a 'free city', the Soviet Union would turn over its Berlin rights to the GDR, a mass panic set in lest the last door to the West should be closed. This panic reached its height between January and August 1961, when an astonishing 181,007 people fled; of these, 48.2 per cent were under the age of 25. In August 1961, the GDR sealed off its borders to the West by erecting a wall through Berlin and putting up formidable fences along the German–German border.

This response to the increasing haemorrhage saved the GDR, but it also represented, literally, the cementing of the two-state status of East and West Germany. The 'Berlin crisis' unleashed by Khrushchev's ultimatum, to which the Western Allies refused to accede, came to a head at Checkpoint Charlie in October 1961 when Soviet and American tanks confronted one another. It ended with the GDR population virtually imprisoned, and hopes of unification further away than ever. In the 1960s, the theme of unification was gradually replaced by that of coming to terms with the apparent *fait accompli* of co-existence. Not political unity, but maintaining links at micro-level, at the level of individuals and their families was what now seemed important. In December 1963, East Germany and the West Berlin Senate reached agreement on permitting visits by West Berliners to relations in East Germany over the Christmas and New Year periods; further agreements followed in subsequent years. Under the 'grand coalition' of CDU and SPD which replaced the CDU government in November 1966, the Hallstein doctrine was gradually abandoned, and diplomatic relations established to Eastern European countries such as Rumania (1967) and Yugoslavia (1968). Gradually, West Germany was coming to accept the reality of the Soviet bloc and the GDR.

THE ADVENT OF *OSTPOLITIK*

In 1969, the SPD under Willy Brandt took over the government of West Germany. The cautious process of appeasement under Georg Kiesinger (CDU head of the grand coalition) was developed under Brandt into a policy of conciliation towards the GDR. While Brandt reiterated on 28 October 1969 the Adenauer position that there would be no recognition of East Germany under international law, he reversed CDU policy by recognizing the existence of the two German states as a given fact. The refusal of the CDU to do this had become, increasingly, an unrealistic pose which excluded any possibility of establishing a *modus vivendi* with the GDR. A new era in German–German relations began, commonly known as *ostpolitik*. This *ostpolitik*, based as it was on realism, was at the same time a *realpolitik*. The aim was peaceful co-existence: the move, in other words, from confrontation to cooperation.

Brandt's offer of negotiations with the GDR was taken up by the SED. Willi Stoph, East German prime minister, met Brandt in Erfurt (East Germany) in March 1970; Stoph was received by Brandt in Kassel (West Germany) in May of the same year. These were the first top-level government meetings between the two states. They paved the way towards the establishment of 'good-neighbourly relations' and a 'normalized' relationship between the FRG and GDR. But of course no major steps could be taken without the consent of Moscow. In August 1970, the Treaty of Moscow was signed between the Federal Republic and the Soviet Union. In it, the co-signatories pledged to respect the integrity of all European states within their existing boundaries, including those between the FRG and GDR, and the Oder–Neiße border with Poland. In December 1970, the inviolability of this boundary was recognized in the Treaty of Warsaw, signed by Poland and the Federal Republic. There was much protest, especially in the CDU, to these Treaties, which indeed represented the first major contractual step towards official acceptance of the post-war *status quo*. Objections to the Basic Treaty between the FRG and GDR, which was eventually signed in East Berlin in December 1972, were even more vehement. In the Treaty, West Germany recognized the GDR's separate identity and equality, but not its identity as a foreign state under international law. The Treaty also included clauses pledging the establishment of good relations and the renunciation of force as a means of resolving conflict.

These treaties were the expression of a general trend towards East–West détente and rapprochement in the 1970s. The GDR found entry to UNESCO in November 1972, and became a member of the UN Economic Commission for Europe in December of that year. It was also in December 1972 that the NATO Council of Ministers decided in principle to establish relations with East Germany. When Belgium established diplomatic relations with the GDR in December 1972, it was the first NATO country to do so; but it was quickly followed by Britain and France in February 1973, and the United States in 1974. On 2 May 1974, the two Germanys established permanent representation in each other's capitals – not full diplomatic relations, but the next best thing. At the Helsinki Conference in 1975, when the two Germanys signed the final act on European security and cooperation, Honecker and Helmut Schmidt, representing their two states, sat virtually side by side, separated only by a staircase, and could be observed chatting.

This was a very different situation from that under Adenauer and Ulbricht. These 'good-neighbourly' relations, in line with which a substantial agreement on improving transit routes between Berlin and West Germany was concluded in November 1978, were put to the test, however, with the 'New Cold War' as of 1979. This was the year of the NATO twin-track agreement, which provided for the stationing of 572 US medium-range missiles in Western Europe, including West Germany. The Soviets marched into Afghanistan and, in January 1980, the American government announced economic and political sanctions against the Soviet Union. Yet despite this poisoned atmosphere, East and West Germany sought to preserve good relations; both countries had acquired a degree of independence from their former Allied overseers, and had discovered that the US–Soviet conflict was, above all, a threat to the two Germanys, which were at the geopolitical forefront of this conflict. In May 1980, meeting at Tito's funeral, Schmidt and Honecker agreed that their states should seek to resist the impact of the Afghanistan crisis. Top-level meetings were demonstratively staged; Schmidt visited the GDR in December 1981, and Honecker, after postponing his trip to the FRG, met Schmidt in East Berlin in September 1983. Helmut Kohl, who became West German chancellor in October 1982, ushering in a new period of CDU government, continued the tradition of *ostpolitik,* albeit with muted enthusiasm. Nevertheless, it was under Kohl that Honecker visited the FRG in September 1987, the first visit to West Germany by an East German head of state. A joint communiqué was issued to the effect that 'never again must war be allowed to emanate from German soil', and there were significant agreements on environmental and scientific cooperation, and on the exchange of information relating to nuclear security. Arguably, Honecker's visit represented the apogee of *ostpolitik*.

It is a much-debated point whether such rapprochement prolonged the life of the GDR, thus delaying its collapse and unification, or whether it by contrast brought about a level of meaningful contact and exchange between the two countries, gradually wearing away the boundaries between them. In favour of the first view, it can be argued that the spirit of mutual tolerance created a sense of the unalterability of the *status quo* and thus restricted the development of opposition in the GDR; it can be argued also that the FRG's payment of considerable credits to the GDR over the years, usually in return for humanitarian concessions (witness Franz Josef Strauß's organization of a billion mark credit in 1983) was a not insignificant factor in propping up the regime and thus protracting its reign. In support of the second view, it can be pointed out that the original and lasting thrust behind *ostpolitik* was the idea that peace in Europe – a necessary basis for prospects of unification – would not be possible without some recognition of post-war realities such as the Oder–Neisse border and the GDR. It can be claimed also that the 'politics of small steps' (Egon Bahr) scuppered attempts by the GDR to create a separate sense of East German national cultural identity, helping to maintain a faint, if not negligible sense of corporate Germanness.

THE GDR OPPOSITION MOVEMENT

The political system in the GDR was characterized by enforced and total alignment. The close links between the official parties and mass organizations resulted not so much in mass participation as in the monopolization of opinion and stifling of all difference. Given such structures, the question arises as to what scope there was for dissension, opposition and resistance, and what role this played in bringing about the *Wende*. The period between 1945 and 1953, when party and mass organizations established their authority, can be described as one in which an increasingly monopolistic socialism was imposed on the East Germans; the gradual closing-down, co-opting or takeover by the SED of non-party-affiliated organizations met with wide-ranging resistance across the party-political spectrum, among the student body, and among staff in the universities. In 1953, it was the turn of the workers to stage a massive demonstration against the SED. 1953 represented the apogee of direct confrontation. There were isolated incidents of open protest in 1956 and again in August 1961, when the Berlin Wall was built; but it was not until 1989 that East Germans were once more to take to the streets in mass protest. The trauma of 1953, and the loss of the option to 'vote with one's feet' in 1961, led to a range of reactions. Many GDR citizens became passive *refuseniks*; others sought a societal niche existence and a retreat into the private sphere, or opted for some form of inner emigration. Writers imposed self-censorship – a fact which even applied to such influential writers as Anna Seghers (cf. Thomaneck 1993).

The consolidation of the GDR led to a considerable degree of accommodation with the system, but it also led to a shifting of oppositional focus from direct confrontation to system-immanent criticism. Knowing it was futile to strive to overturn the SED, there was still the hope it could be reformed from within. The shift to system-immanent criticism meant that opposition in the GDR came to be identified with those who supported a reformed or 'humane' socialism. Individuals such as social theorist Wolfgang Harich, publisher Walter Janka, scientist Robert Havemann, critical communist functionary Rudolf Bahro and song-writer Wolf Biermann (cf. Fogg 1984) played a role in drawing attention to the need for reform. Criticism became focused on the SED's lack of commitment to its socialist remit. When Robert Havemann stressed the importance of dialectical processes for all advances in the theory of knowledge (identity and continuity, quantity and quality, being and appearance, unity and difference), he was implicitly attacking the increasing dogmaticism in the state's perception and practice of dialectical materialism (cf. Neubert 1997: 156). The insistence of young Christians and conscientious objectors as of the mid-1960s on the right to a truly non-military form of alternative to military service, and the objections to an increasing militarization of society, exposed inconsistencies within the official position of commitment to peace.

Rudolf Bahro's *The Alternative*

The history of the system-immanent opposition in the GDR has been charted elsewhere (cf. Woods 1986). What this section aims to do is to illustrate by the example of one important reformer, Rudolf Bahro, that there was a theoretical and intellectual model for the transformation of real-existing socialism, a model which can be directly linked to developments in the opposition movement in the 1980s.

Bahro, born in 1935, studied Moral Philosophy at the Humboldt University in Berlin. He was involved for the SED in the process of land collectivization; he held a high position in the trade union administration; he was deputy editor-in-chief of *Forum,* the GDR journal for young people and the intelligentsia, and he worked in industry. In late 1976, Bahro put the finishing touches to his book *The Alternative* (*Die Alternative*), hailed by Herbert Marcuse as the most important contribution to Marxist theory and practice to appear in decades (Marcuse 1978: 5). In it, Bahro presented an anti-SED view, arguing that the Eastern bloc was being run by fossilized castes preventing the emergence of socialism. The managerial and executive pyramid, Bahro maintained, is dominated by vertical, hierarchical and authority-orientated nodes rather than horizontal ones at the base. Attempts to involve mass initiative, such as competitions between brigades, the idea of the 'innovators' movement' (*Neuererbewegung*), and bonus systems, Bahro adjudged to be fraught with bureaucratic controls, thus contributing to rather than counteracting the feeling of dissatisfaction in the production process (Bahro 1977: 75). Nor did Bahro stop short of a radical demontage of the SED and CPSU, in whose bureaucratic apparatus he saw only a mechanism of consolidating existing power relations.

Bahro was not pessimistic, however. He believed an 'alternative', i.e. true socialism, to be growing in the womb of 'actually existing socialism' or 'proto-socialism'. Bahro's hope was that the existing party and its apparatus could be overthrown by a comprehensive cultural revolution, triggered by the conspiratorial formation of a new communist party under the old nineteenth-century name of 'League of Communists' (Bahro 1977: 410f). Bahro defined socialism in terms of Marxist ideology, presenting his critique of 'actually existing socialism' within the framework of Marxism-Leninism (Bahro 1977: 24f). But his Marxism adapted Marxist theory in line with new developments such as the bureaucratization of modern life and the contradictions of the north–south and east–west axes (Bahro 1977: 35).

According to Bahro, progressive ideas can never be developed by the essentially conservative working classes, and the trade unions never anticipate a new culture. With the rejection of the Marxist role of the working classes, there arose the quest for a new revolutionary subject. In six lectures summarizing the ideas contained in *Die Alternative,* Bahro argued that the 'source of movement' which would overcome the existing situation would be made up of the 'creative elements' in all areas of society (Bahro 1979: 25). Effectively, Bahro propagated the leadership role of the intellectual in Gramsci's meaning of the word, i.e. of people who reflect on social problems and socio-theoretical issues in direct contact to the basis, resulting in a redefinition of both basis and intellectual and in the establishment of direct democracy (Bahro, Mandel and von Oertzen 1980: 130f).

Bahro's criticism of 'actually existing socialism' was fundamental. He argued that the latter could not facilitate the development of the individual, for rather than initiating the decline of the state as a representative institution, it had strengthened it, and rather than initiating the abolition of the traditional division of labour, it had consolidated it. Concomitantly, subalternity was the rule in the iron cage of bureaucratization and party apparatus dominance. Among the results were a stifling of initiative and total alienation, with a resultant enhanced desire for material goods pandered to by the party leadership. Bahro's fundamental critique of 'actually existing socialism' constituted in the first instance a total rejection of Honecker's consumerist policy of the so-called unity of economic and social policy (cf. McCauley 1981: 3–20, and Jarausch 1998: 33–46). But it also signified a complete overhaul of Marxist orthodox theory, with the emphasis on the regenerative role of intellectuals as movers towards a new socialist future. It was this clarion call to the intellectuals which was to become reality in the GDR during the 1980s.

Opposition and unification: contradictions?

The 1980s, as Fulbrook observed (Fulbrook 1991: 266), brought with them a proliferation of dissent in the GDR, which built on the principle of system-immanent criticism. Discrepancies between the GDR's official line on peace, the environment and human rights (which it had pledged to respect at Helsinki in 1975) and an ever more divergent practice became the source of criticism from a widening number and range of opposition groups. For the first time, some of these groups were set up and even to an extent operated outside of the Church. Within the Church, too, there was diversification as the 'Church from Below' called for a more radically critical Church stance. Demarcation lines between groups became less well defined as there was increasing understanding that peace, human rights and the environment were interrelated issues. This became particularly clear in the wake of the Chernobyl disaster. Collaborative networks were set up, such as 'Taking Concrete Steps for Peace' (*Konkret für den Frieden*) in 1983, or 'The Initiative for Peace and Human Rights' (IFM) in 1986, which strove to set up a GDR-wide information network across various peace, ecology and human rights groupings, helping to overcome boundaries. The Environment Library, founded in 1986 in Berlin, was a similarly broad-based informational venture. Increasingly, too, it became clear to opposition groups not only that all the issues on their agendas were interrelated, but also, and more explosively, that this inherent connectedness required radical structural solutions at both national and international level. In the course of the 1980s, as the nuclear threat increased, and especially after it seemed that reform in the Soviet Union was a real possibility, some GDR intellectuals and members of opposition groups began to suggest solutions whose international boldness flew in the face of the more cautious and apparently realistic politics being pursued by Bonn and East Berlin.

Prior to the 1980s, the GDR peace movement had largely directed its criticism towards the military character of life, particularly within education, in the GDR. In the 1980s, there were increased calls for the de-militarization of the two Germanys, and of Europe as a whole. The idea of creating an 'atomic-weapons-free zone' within Europe by removing nuclear weapons bilaterally within agreed areas on both sides of the Iron Curtain was an idea taken up by Honecker in the 1980s and discussed in various SED–SPD meetings, such as that in September 1985. Here, the GDR government and the peace movement shared similar beliefs, at least on paper. Neither this idea, nor the more radical one of creating a 'block-free zone' by taking countries out of the NATO and Warsaw Pact structures as a prerequisite for a lasting de-escalation, was first thought of in the GDR. But the notion of freeing up zones on either side of the East–West divide was very vigorously championed by the GDR opposition movement. Throughout the 1980s, during the numerous Peace Decades and other multifarious peace gatherings, peace groups asked not just for a proper alternative to military service or for an end to defence studies in schools in the GDR, but also stressed the need for far-reaching international solutions to the nuclear threat and the military bloc system.

While the impetus for this trend came from general developments such as the deployment of medium-range missiles, there was a specific impetus too. This was the East German 'Berlin Appeal' of 25 January 1982, which had been initiated by parson Rainer Eppelmann and the socialist intellectual Robert Havemann – a significant example of church–intelligentsia cooperation. Eighty signatories put their names to the Appeal, the *leitmotiv* of which was the GDR peace movement's slogan 'Creating peace without weapons'. The Appeal called for Europe to be declared an atomic-weapons-free zone, arguing that both German governments should negotiate on the bilateral removal of weapons from their countries. But it went further than this. Pointing out that divided Germany had become a kind of parade-ground for both atomic superpowers, it suggested that the Allies conclude a peace treaty with the two Germanys, withdraw their troops and guarantee non-intervention in the inner affairs of both states (Neubert 1997: 408f). Only in the later part of the Appeal were there the usual references to the need for a social peace service in the GDR and an end to defence studies. Havemann, Eppelmann and their co-signatories perhaps demonstrated little sense of political pragmatism, but they exhibited a visionary zeal and a balanced awareness of the source of the problem, resisting any temptation to blame one side or the other. And they dared to connect the peace question with the German question and even touched on the sensitive issue of self-determination.

Some examples will serve to illustrate the broader political contextualization of the peace issue which followed in the wake of the Berlin Appeal. According to SED Central Committee sources, the Peace Decade in 1983 was typified by a variety of protest. In Forst, one

Peter Müller told some 100 to 200 youngsters who attended a meeting in church rooms on 7 November 1983 that they should insist on their right to refuse military service and on the introduction of a social peace service. In Finsterwalde, during a youth workshop-cum-religious service attended by some 400 people, a letter to Honecker was read out pointing to apparent contradictions between the GDR's commitment to peace and its political practice. These two cases illustrate domestic and national criticism. In the *Weinbergskirche* in Dresden on 9 November 1983, however, people were asked to sign a resolution which contained demands for 'German–German rapprochement', as well as protesting against the stationing of rockets in both West Germany and the GDR. Throughout the GDR, a number of clerics spoke out in their sermons against 'the arms race in East and West', saying that 'the source of the evil is to be found not just in the West, but in the East'. In 1985, the Peace Decade also connected criticism of the SED with a call for international responses. Again according to official Central Committee reports, the critical substance of the various meetings focused on the lack of human rights and right to travel in GDR, on restrictions on GDR citizens to develop their personalities, on lack of transparency in power structures and on military service. But there were also calls for 'a peace movement across the military blocs', for 'personal peace treaties' between GDR citizens and citizens in non-socialist countries, and, given the fact that 'one cannot rely on the mighty any more', for 'peace from below', an idea which had been in currency since 1983.

While much of this still sounded vague, the arrival of IFM on the GDR's oppositional scene in the mid-1980s and of their publication *GRENZFALL* – literally 'falling of boundaries' – provided momentum. One of IFM's declared aims was to work towards an end of the military bloc system, the removal of nuclear weapons within certain zones, which would then be neutral, and towards an end, as a result of this process, to German division. On the Day of Human Rights in the *Gethsemanekirche* (East Berlin), which took place on 10 December 1987, IFM issued a statement reinforcing its commitment to the process of 'ending the division of Europe decided on in Yalta', and expressing its support of a political policy aimed at 'the dissolution of the two blocs and the overcoming of this division'. According to IFM, aspects of this policy are the 'CSCE process, and the idea of atomic-weapons-free, demilitarized or neutralized zones' (IFM 1987: 131–33). There was some shifting of ground in the question of emphasis among opposition groups. When, in 1985, the Czech opposition group Charta 77 issued an appeal to allow Germans their unity, a number of GDR reformers responded on 8 June 1985 with a statement basically saying 'yes' to the idea of a peace treaty with both German states, but stressing that the German question can only play a role 'embedded in a set of treaties involving the whole of Europe' (Poppe 1995: 268). The basic problem was deciding whether to put the German question at the beginning of a process of de-escalation, with a neutral and perhaps even united Germany leading the way, or right at the end, as the final stage in a contractually agreed and staged process of overcoming the confrontation of the two blocs.

The idea of ending division was, then, very much on the opposition's agenda. True, there was the inherent dilemma that overcoming division might mean an end to the socialist project. In its 10 December 1987 declaration, IFM stressed that what was wanted in the GDR was democratization (civil rights, democratic controls, independent courts, administrative jurisdiction, end to violation of private sphere), while pointing out that what was *not* wanted was Western-style parliamentary democracy, but a democratization with a true chance for 'social self-administration' (IFM 1987: 133). Whether this would be possible in a united Germany was highly questionable. It was awareness of this dilemma that led to a degree of ambivalence vis-à-vis unification among some members of the opposition movement, and to the strong stance taken against Kohl-style unification in 1989/1990. Others, however, such as Rainer Eppelmann, were not at all ambivalent. A paper drawn up by Eppelmann in 1987 ends with the quotation: 'the German question is open as long as the Brandenburg Gate is closed!'. In the final analysis, what mattered in the 1980s was the GDR opposition movement's broad commitment to the process of peace within Europe and particularly between the two Germanys, and to the ideal of ending divisions. This commitment was a vital factor in making both the *Wende* and the mass support for unification possible, however the opposition felt when unification was actually on the cards.

RHETORIC AND REALITY: THE UNBRIDGED GULF

Faced with the constant westward movement of many of its citizens, with the effects of *ostpolitik*, mounting opposition and increasing economic problems in the 1980s, what efforts did the SED make to rescue the socialist project? The remainder of this chapter focuses on the trade union movement, and argues that, while efforts were made to integrate the workers to a greater degree in decision-making, these efforts often remained rhetorical, thus increasing rather than allaying grass-roots dissatisfaction.

According to its own propaganda, the political system in the GDR was based on democratic participation, realized by the policy of alliance for the purpose of overcoming the class-division of society. The multi-party system, the mass organizations and professional organizations played an important role in this policy. As well as their role in lobbying, they had a mobilizing role for the achievement of a permanent revolutionary process. The SED's closest ally among the mass organizations was the Free German Trade Union (FDGB) with over 9 million members. The role of the trade unions in the GDR, and in particular the relationship between the FDGB and the SED, were very clearly defined. The FDGB saw itself as an instrument for the realization of the decisions taken by the SED. By 1948, even before the SED declared itself a party of the 'new type', the FDGB had acknowledged the primacy of the SED and had *de facto* become a Leninist trade union movement (Thomaneck 1990). Subsequently the FDGB made a major contribution to the implementation of the SED's economic and social policy and to the GDR's internal stability. It was through the FDGB that the SED established its power base, and at the same time projected an image of participatory socialism.

This image was conveyed with particular force during the Honecker era. At the 8th SED Party Congress of 1971, the task was set of raising the material and cultural living conditions in the GDR by rapid expansion of socialist production, increases in efficiency, and scientific–technological progress. Within this context, the trade union movement was officially to be accorded a new status. In a lecture in March 1973, the then leader of the FDGB Herbert Warnke criticized Ulbricht's policies and heralded a new trade union era (Warnke 1977: 275). It was to be marked by a tripartite relationship between government, SED and FDGB, and by greater participation in economic management and planning. After 1971, references to this tripartite relationship abounded in official decrees and proclamations, appearing time and again, for instance, in Honecker's speeches.

In contrast to other mass organizations, the status of the FDGB was enshrined in the 1968 GDR constitution (revised in 1974). Thus Article 45 laid down the bargaining rights of the trade unions, and their right to initiate legislation. Paragraph 3 also enshrined the responsibility of the trade unions for administering the national insurance scheme. Paragraph 4 obliged all state and economic agencies to cooperate with the trade unions. But the new status of the trade unions was to go beyond these provisions. They were to be the key agents in the construction of socialism at both macro- and microeconomic levels. Coresponsibility, codetermination and cooperation were the official catchwords. The message sent by the SED Central Committee to the 11th FDGB Congress in 1987 emphasized that 'the trade unions were, are, and shall remain the decisive factor in the functioning of our socialist democracy' (FDGB 1987: 5f). However, the embedding of the trade unions in the body politic as part of the tripartite relationship was criticized in the West. It was rightly argued that the GDR trade unions were not really trade unions, and certainly not free trade unions, because the FDGB acknowledged the primacy of the SED. It was also pointed out that the FDGB was no more than a state union. The FDGB fully acknowledged this position to its peril.

The proclaimed enhanced public role of the FDGB went hand in hand, however, with a not always unjustified criticism of the West. The GDR shared a border with the Federal Republic of Germany which was very much the shop window of capitalism. It was not surprising that the GDR authorities no longer attempted to counteract the attraction of capitalism by promising greater material wealth, as during the Ulbricht era, choosing instead to draw attention to the exemplary social safety net and absence of unemployment in the GDR.

By the early 1980s, it was becoming clear that Honecker's policy of the 'unity of economic and social policy' was not working out. To sustain it, vast, crippling foreign debts were being incurred. Problems and imminent failure were not only discernible at the macro-economic level. The manuscript of a speech written for delivery at a Trade Union Conference on 3 December 1982 referred to an ever-increasing productivity gap, stressing that, while capitalist countries were achieving new productivity rates of between 20 and 25 per cent as a result of large research and rationalization programmes, the GDR could only manage a rate of 8 per cent. It also pointed to the difficulty of producing high-quality goods in order to compete at realistic price levels in the world market. Further highlighted in the manuscript was the difficulty of coping with increasing interest rates for foreign credits and maintaining the level of imports for public consumption.

In this context of deepening economic crisis – symptomatic of which was the fact that *per capita* output in the GDR was half that of the FRG – productivity was to be increased by the intensified application of high technology. The consequences of greater rationalization, increased efficiency and use of high technology for the workforce and trade unions are well known in the West. While loss of jobs was not one of them in the GDR, there was a steady increase in multi-shift working between 1980 and 1983, while the number of people working in a one or two-shift system decreased. More efficient utilization of equipment, the avoidance of waste, recycling, and the refinement of raw materials were of paramount importance for keeping production costs down, especially in the GDR, which was singularly short of raw materials and dependent on imports.

In the late 1980s, the GDR stepped up its campaign for modernization even more. The parameters for achieving this great 'leap forward' were set out in the 1986–1990 Five Year Plan Act, which outlined that high-technology industries would have to be developed and used at an accelerated pace.

The SED expected the FDGB leaders to sweeten the bitter pill of increased productivity, more shift work, and greater quality control by stressing that human creativity would be enhanced as a result of the new technologies. The technological leap forward would obviously require a highly trained workforce to ensure appropriate involvement in preplanning, application of plans, consultation with management, and evaluation of research. Correspondingly, increasing the level of education and qualification would lead to a desire for greater participation and codetermination. According to the Five Year Plan, the trade unions were to have an important role in this area of socialist democracy. Moreover, it was stressed that innovation could not be left to arise out of serendipity. Teams of innovators comprising researchers, technicians, and workers would need to be formed to make possible a more integrated and efficient organization. This in itself would increase participation for all, helping towards the abolition of the division of labour into creative and less creative jobs. Again, the trade unions as the organizing motor of the 'innovators' movement' would have a crucial role to play. Such an organizational form of work collectives would become more common and cut across the traditional organization of work brigades.

In 1989, there were plans to force the pace of modernization even more when, for the first time in the GDR, a separate plan for investments was worked out, closely related to the material plan for science and technology. 76 billion East German marks were to be invested to enhance the technological and material basis of the economy. Eighty per cent of investment was to be in technology. Three hundred projects focused on the development and application of microelectronics, the extension of the energy sector, the GDR's export potential, working and living conditions and the protection of the environment. Fifty-nine projects aimed at improving efficiency in the supply industries, the provision of consumer goods, and the quality of export articles.

By 1989, this drive had taken on a somewhat frenzied, desperate character. The situation within GDR industry was a cause for concern. Problems of which the SED was aware were: the issue of *refuseniks*; lack of motivation; an information and technology gap; a lack of participatory democracy in the workplace and in decision-making processes; inadequate involvement of young people; and the moribund state of the economy (cf. Kuhrt, Buck and Holzweißig 1996). Arguably, it was not just the lack of actual grass-roots influence in GDR industry which frustrated the workers, but also the increasingly obvious discrepancy between proclaimed industrial advance and actual stagnation. Despite the greater emphasis placed on trade unions by Honecker, despite the talk of an 'emancipated' workforce working harmoniously with technology in the 1980s, socialist democracy and codetermination were never perceived by the working population to be a reality. The close links to the GDR's political and state machinery gradually wore away the FDGB's credibility. In October 1989, the working population of the GDR showed they had not accepted the official notion of socialist democracy and the proclaimed transfer of power to the rank and file.

5   The events of 1989/1990

THE MISMANAGEMENT OF CRISIS

That Honecker's attempt at political crisis management and linguistic 'democracy' camouflage had failed became clear in the autumn of 1989, when the working people reminded him: 'We are the people'. Whereas the Polish free trade union *Solidarity* movement did not in any noticeable way capture the mood of the working people in the GDR, the policy shifts announced by Mikhail Gorbachev after his appointment as General Secretary of the Communist Party of the Soviet Union in 1985 triggered a new political discourse in East Germany. Gorbachev realized that the system of 'actually existing socialism' simply could not continue, either in the Soviet Union or in the Eastern bloc as a whole. He launched his programme of openness (*glasnost*), reform (*perestroika*) and non-interference in other aligned countries in his 'Political Report of the CPSU Central Committee to the 27th Party Congress' on 25 February 1986 (cf. Gorbachev 1996). The intellectuals, managers, and ordinary people of East Germany saw Gorbachev and his policies as a panacea for the ills of the GDR regime. The new socialist theory exposed the contradictions in the GDR body politic and increased the awareness of an intolerable gap between the officially propagated image and actual existing reality.

The GDR regime was not only aware of its economic plight, it was also fully aware of the impact of Gorbachev's new policies on the citizens of its state. It appeared unable to make up its mind how to react to this impact. In an interview with the West German illustrated weekly *Der Stern,* the GDR chief ideologue Kurt Hager stated on 9 April 1987 in respect of Gorbachev's reforms: 'Would you, when your neighbour puts new wallpaper up in his flat, feel obliged to put up new wallpaper in yours?' Hager's statement, with the politburo's backing, was printed in *Neues Deutschland* the following day, and triggered a wave of protest letters within the GDR, not least from the SED basis itself (Wolle 1998: 292). Yet, in an unexpected gesture towards *glasnost*, the SED allowed and even officially accompanied a massive peace demonstration in September 1987, when the official East German 'Peace Council' and the Free German Youth Movement joined peace-committed and reform-minded groups of Christians on the Olof-Palme peace walk from Ravensbrück to Sachsenhausen concentration-camp memorial sites. The reformers carried placards calling for 'Free contacts to East and West', 'Peace education instead of defence studies' and 'Swords to ploughshares'. It was the first permitted demonstration in the GDR. 'New possibilities have opened up', wrote the editors of the samisdat newspaper *Umweltblätter* in October 1987, 'possibilities which must be built on by the peace movement'.

Ultimately, however, the SED decided to resist all calls for reform, not to enter into dialogue with reformers, and to stifle all critical voices. The decision was a mistake, because dissatisfaction had now reached such a level that every act of state repression led to a redoubling of protest, intensifying the mood of discontent. In November 1987, the Stasi stormed the *Zionskirche* rooms of the Environment Library and arrested a number of those responsible for publishing the critical circular *GRENZFALL*. When about 200 people protested against these arrests, they too were taken into custody. But a new group of protesters took their place, and when the Western media took interest in the conflict, the authorities were forced to back down and release those imprisoned. The Environment Library 'affair' led many dissatisfied GDR citizens, including exit visa applicants, to gather in the *Zionskirche*, and for 17 January 1988 – the occasion of official commemoration of the murder of the distinguished communist leaders Rosa Luxemburg and Karl Liebknecht – members of the GDR opposition and exit visa applicants planned to stage a common protest by taking part in the demonstration with their own banners and placards demanding *glasnost*, peace, and tolerance. 120 demonstrators were arrested. On 30 January, 1,500 people in the *Gethsemanekirche* in East Berlin participated in a prayer service for those arrested. A week later, this figure had reached 2,000.

A further example of the 'redoubling' effect came later in the year. When 37 schoolchildren at the Carl-von-Ossietzky School in Berlin put their signatures to a petition calling for an end to military parades on the GDR's National Holiday, they were subjected to massive pressure to withdraw their names. But five remained steadfast, and on 14 October 1988 they were expelled. On 19 November 1988, the SED banned the Soviet publication *Sputnik*, which had helped to convey some of the ideas of Gorbachev. There then followed on 20 November a GDR-wide action, initiated in the Berlin Church *Erlöserkirche*, in protest at the expulsion, and calling for more pluralism and democracy.

In addition to stifling protest, the SED pursued a policy of promising concessions and then backpedalling, a policy which could also be counterproductive. Despite Gorbachev, all forms of public dissemination of literary material were still subject to strict bureaucratic controls at different levels within the political hierarchy. Encouraged by *glasnost*, East German writers in the late 1980s began to protest openly against censorship. The Writers' Union at meetings in 1985, 1986 and 1987 had to deal with complaints from writers in respect of censorship, particularly in relation to television, but also the theatre. At the 24 June 1987 meeting, dramatist Peter Brasch reported that, in the Academy of Arts, a committee had been set up to represent the 'interests' of dramatists vis-à-vis the Ministry for Culture – such was the degree of discontent. Problems of censorship were a central theme of the 1987 10th Writers' Congress, especially in the workshop moderated by the author Christoph Hein, which dealt with the relationship between literature and society. The effect of Hein's criticism of censorship at this workshop (he was ably seconded by author Günter de Bruyn) was to trigger prospects of a more relaxed cultural policy on the part of the SED. Censorship boss Klaus Höpcke promised in a meeting of the Writers' Union *Präsidium* on 28 June 1988 that a draft for new 'permission to print procedures' was to be discussed by the *Volkskammer*. According to the draft, publishers would in future only have to submit their decision to publish together with their reasons, but not the manuscript, nor any of the notorious reports on the manuscript. The writer Volker Braun, in a moment of extreme optimism, described this draft as an 'exemplary illustration of the redistribution of power' and as 'socialist democracy in action'.

Despite these moves, the SED continued to make life difficult for authors, including Hein and Volker Braun. Perceiving Hein's play *Die Ritter der Tafelrunde*, which portrays the collapse of the Arthurian Round Table, to be an attack on the SED, the authorities obstructed its first performance. Eventually it was performed in Dresden in the form of a 'Pre-performance' on 24 March 1989, the premiere being delayed till 12 April. The neurotic reaction to Hein's play on the part of officialdom, however, merely attracted public attention to it, and when it was revived during the *Wende*, it was this very neurotic reaction which predetermined its reception as an anti-SED play. Far from prohibiting the play's critical effect, the authorities had unwittingly supported it.

In addition to repression, bans, empty rhetoric and promises, the SED and Stasi had planned tougher measures, such as 'isolating' potential sources of unrest. According to the GDR's last Chief Public Prosecutioner, 10,918 people were targeted for isolation throughout the GDR in November 1988. Plans for isolation date back to Mielke's directive Nr. 1/67 from July 1967, which states categorically that 'individuals and groups are to be isolated whose political reliability in a situation of defence is not guaranteed and in whose case there is good reason to suspect that they could have (...) a negative political and ideological influence'. This directive, supplemented by further directives between 1984 and 1985, was intended for implementation in a 'period of tension', understood officially as a period preceding the outbreak of international conflict. But clearly the elasticity of the concept 'period of tension' meant that, effectively, the GDR opposition movement lived for at least 2 decades not just under the threat of expulsion and imprisonment, but also under that of 'isolation'. During the 40 years' anniversary celebrations in October 1989, the Stasi and police had orders to keep tight controls at the border to West Berlin in case of West German interference, and also, where necessary, to intern or isolate 'negative' groups and individuals. Thus the security plan 'Jubilee 40' issued on 8 September 1989 by the head of the Regional Stasi Administration in Berlin includes a reference to Order No. 051/85 of the Minister of the Interior, the update of 051/84, a directive governing internment and isolation.

The Stasi had mapped out a whole network of 'isolation objects' throughout the GDR to be filled in case of 'emergency'. Local Stasi branches were entrusted with finding suitable 'objects' and drawing up lists of potential 'isolees'. Thus by February 1987, the Stasi responsible for the Erfurt area had drawn up a list of 905 people who were to be 'secured' in a range of buildings including a children's home in Heiligenstadt, a restaurant in Sondershausen, a hotel in Weimar, and – more basic – a builders' hut in Eisenach. That isolation was not necessarily going to be an entirely painless process is made clear from the occasional use of the word 'liquidation' in Stasi documentation relating to the subject. That it did not come to such isolation or annihilation was a direct result of the enormity and peacefulness of the revolutionary process.

THE *WENDE*

Throughout 1988 and early 1989, protest and repression, calls for reform and refusal followed one another in increasingly tense succession. On 13 February 1989 a demonstration in Dresden for human rights, and for freedom of speech and press was forcibly dissolved by the police. On 19 February, Western journalists were prevented from recording the proceedings of the Protestant Synod in Saxony. In May 1989, on the occasion of the visit of the Soviet Minister of Defence, Honecker took a stance against Gorbachev's policy of non-interference in the affairs of Eastern bloc states by calling for a strengthening of the Warsaw Pact. And on 19 January 1989, Honecker proclaimed that the Berlin Wall would still exist in 50, even a 100 years. This statement stood in stark contrast to Gorbachev's idea of a 'common European house' signalling the end of the Cold War between the two power blocs. It also signalled to reformers in the GDR that the SED politburo would not entertain a new political discourse. This became spectacularly evident on the occasion of the local government elections of 7 May 1989, which were not only 'staged' in the usual manner, but also shown to have involved clear instances of falsifying results. Spontaneous demonstrations ensued, and the Protestant Church demanded changes to the electoral law and greater protection of citizen rights by law. Internationally, the GDR leadership sought the friendship of Rumania's hated dictator Ceaucescu, and in June 1989 politburo member Egon Krenz expressed the politburo's solidarity with the Chinese leadership, which had brutally suppressed demonstrations by students and intellectuals in Beijing.

The politburo displayed all the symptoms of a fortress mentality, leading to further alienation, even among its own party members. According to the secretariat of the Egon Krenz Office on 18 January 1989, 23,000 internal party trials were conducted against party members in 1988, the highest number since the 8th Party Conference. A memorandum from the secretariat reads: 'There has been an increase in the number of members and candidates who had to be removed from the party because they opposed the general line, denied the successes of the GDR, constantly carped and complained, or betrayed the party'. 11,084 party penalties were levied on account of 'violations of Leninist norms', and 4,425 of these penalties involved exclusion from the SED. In 1988, 834 SED members did not return from trips to West Germany, as contrasted with 424 in 1987; 1,135 members applied for an exit visa. Party members increasingly called for greater pluralism, basing their calls on reformist Soviet publications such as *Sputnik*.

The degree of alienation was demonstrated by the incipient break-up of the monolithic structures of the Central Committee and even the politburo itself, where individuals began to question the sustainability of the fortress mentality espoused by Honecker and the majority of the 'old guard'. It was also demonstrated by the fact that, during the first 6 months of 1989, over 46,000 GDR citizens left the country legally, while thousands left illegally via the West German embassies in Prague and Warsaw, or via Hungary, which in May had relaxed its border controls with Austria; on 11 September, it finally opened its borders to Austria for East German emigrants. This step was taken by the Hungarian Socialist authorities days after the Hungarian Prime Minister Niklos Nemeth and Foreign Minister Gyula Horn had met with Federal Chancellor Helmut Kohl and Foreign Minister Hans-Dietrich Genscher in Bonn. This 4-hour meeting resulted in a communiqué which said little about the actual discussions, but clearly the opening of the Hungarian border was decided upon. It was the first instance in the context of the *Wende* where Helmut Kohl and Genscher took the initiative and can be credited with decisive action contributing to the collapse of the GDR.

However, the major actions of the *Wende* were still initiated by the protest movement inside the GDR. An ever-increasing number of people were taking to the streets, especially in Saxony. Originating in the churches and carried by intellectuals, these demonstrations became a regular occurrence. By 9 October 1989, the Monday demonstration in Leipzig attracted 70,000 people, the one in Dresden 12,000. Dissidence and opposition had reached the masses. The dominant slogans of these demonstrations were 'We are the people' and 'We are staying here', indicating the demand for reform, highlighting the vast gulf between the politburo and the people, and the fact that demonstrators wanted to revolutionize the GDR from within. At this time formal groupings, associations, and parties emerged without the approval of the authorities. The first and most important was 'New Forum' (*Neues Forum*), founded by the painter Bärbel Bohley and the writer Jens Reich on 10 September 1989. Others such as 'Democracy Now' (*Demokratie Jetzt*) followed. Intellectuals were establishing an alternative party system.

In the context of the above events, the SED staged the official celebrations for the 40th anniversary of the GDR. Gorbachev attended these celebrations, in fact his poster was carried by many demonstrators as a sign of protest against the Honecker regime and a symbol of hope. Never had an official act of self-congratulation in the GDR had as hollow a ring as this one. The revolutionary movement was encouraged by Gorbachev's public withdrawal of support for Honecker. His somewhat loosely translated statement made at this time spread like wildfire: 'He who is too late will be punished by life'. The question remained as to whether the Honecker regime would suppress the popular movement by using military force. The turning point was the Leipzig demonstration of 9 October when, due largely to the endeavours of Kurt Masur (the conductor of the Leipzig *Gewandhaus* orchestra), the very likely-seeming escalation was miraculously avoided. Regional SED officials in Leipzig refused the further use of force after a meeting with Masur. The slogan 'No violence' shouted by the demonstrators had, it seemed, impressed itself upon the authorities.

This also sealed Honecker's fate. On 18 October, he resigned. His 'crown prince' Egon Krenz succeeded him in all his dictatorial functions. However, Krenz proclaimed a *Wende* of the SED towards a dialogue with the people. A fortnight later he promised a great socialist renewal. But Krenz and the existing politburo did not enjoy even a modicum of trust; too many empty promises had been made for too long. The demonstrations continued to grow and spread. On 23 October, 300,000 people took to the streets in Leipzig, expressing their disapproval of Krenz's appointment. Then, on 4 November 1989, more than half a million people gathered on the Alexanderplatz in East Berlin to listen to leading intellectuals such as the writers Christa Wolf and Stefan Heym, and to demand free elections and true democracy. The new regime's appeasement policy concentrated on the issue of more liberal travel legislation, but by this stage the Krenz administration was staggering far behind ever more rapid developments in the political consciousness of the majority of GDR citizens. On 6 November, a law was proclaimed giving every citizen the right to travel abroad as a private person, on business, or on a permanent basis. One day later the cabinet announced its intention to resign; on the following day, the politburo resigned. The new-look politburo no longer included hard-liners. On 9 November, the cabinet decided to open the GDR's borders to the West. Millions of East Germans began to cross the border. An effective passport or identity card control became impossible. Soon the world saw people from East and West dancing on the Berlin Wall.

ON THE ROAD TO UNITY

The world was taken by surprise, and the significance of the fall of the Wall not immediately appreciated. Six days later, the British Foreign

Minister Douglas Hurd stated after talks with the West German Foreign Minister that the issue of unification was not topical. But in the GDR itself, those reformers who had paved the way for the *Wende* began to fear a Western capitalist takeover. On 28 November, a large number of intellectuals, writers and artists in the GDR issued a proclamation 'For our country', calling for the continuation of a (new, humanized) GDR, while in the streets, GDR citizens began to articulate visions of a united Germany, calling out 'We are one people' and 'Germany, united fatherland'. Chancellor Helmut Kohl proved himself to be more in tune with such visions than the new SED leadership, or for that matter than the intellectual leaders of East Germany's 'gentle revolution'. Also on 28 November, he proposed to the West German *Bundestag* a ten-point-programme to overcome the division of Germany. The programme proposed the abolition of the SED monopoly on power, democratic and economic renewal, and a confederative structure encompassing both states. The long-term aim would be the unification of Germany.

Kohl's reading of the situation and timing certainly were astute and remarkable. Nevertheless, the epithet 'Chancellor of Unity' with which it has become customary to describe Kohl is an overstatement. He did not seem to have had any long-term plan for unification; action on the German question developed according to political factors prevailing at any one time. Moreover, according to the historian Gerhard Wettig (Wettig 1998: 86), as late as December 1989 the Chancellor still believed it would take more than 4 or 5 years to achieve unification – despite his proposed ten-point plan. The media image of the 'Chancellor of Unity' proved particularly galling for the intellectual leaders of the *Wende* and the people in the GDR generally, because their role was underplayed as a result. What has been forgotten is not only that the GDR reformers made the *Wende* possible, but also that often they were not against unification *per se*, at least not as a long-term goal, but against unification on the terms of the FRG. Subsequently accused of having misjudged the mood of the people, of a lack of national pride, and even of Stalinist loyalties, the GDR's former opposition movement has, arguably, continued to be marginalized as much after 1990 as before under the SED.

The fate of the intellectual leaders in terms of political influence was finally sealed by the elections of March 1990, the first and last free parliamentary elections in the GDR. These elections also pushed the SED (now PDS) aside as a leading political force. The SED had become further discredited from late 1989 onwards when disclosures of relatively paltry corruption on the part of some of its leading mem-

bers enraged the GDR populace. The vast majority of the former
politburo members were expelled from the SED, and some of them
were placed for a while under house arrest, including Honecker. Egon
Krenz resigned on 6 December as Head of the Presidential Council
and the Defence Council. Hans Modrow was appointed Prime
Minister. He initiated a number of reforms, and showed willingness
to involve the new parties and the churches in a process of dialogue
and cooperation. This process was furthered by 'Round Table talks'.
At the first of these on 7 December 1989, it had been agreed that a new
constitution be worked out, and that parliamentary elections be held
on 6 May 1990. Because of the will of the demonstrating populace,
whose prime objective now appeared to be unification, this date was
changed to 18 March.

On 5 February, a new GDR government was formed, including
eight members of the opposition parties. On 20 February, Modrow
declared himself in favour of negotiations with the aim of German
unification. This change in attitude resulted largely from an awareness of the imminent collapse of the East German economy. The
results of the election of 18 March represented a clear vote for unification. The conservative Alliance for Germany (consisting of CDU,
DSU and Democratic Awakening) gained 47.7 per cent of the votes,
the SPD 21.8 per cent, the PDS 16.3 per cent, the Liberals 5.3 per
cent and *Bündnis 90* (an alliance of GDR reform groups) a mere 2.9
per cent. The election results also represented a victory for West
German parties. The East German CDU had become an adjunct
of the West German CDU, the SPD an adjunct of the West
German SPD, and the liberal parties' liaison had aligned itself to
the West German FDP. These parties were financed in their campaigns by their Western counterparts, and the major speakers of the
campaign were West German party luminaries. In fact the elections
looked like West German elections fought in a strangely unreal geographical and socio-economic context. The indigenous parties and
party groupings like the German Social Union (DSU) and *Bündnis
90* achieved no more than splinter party status. Indigenous political
life had been terminated.

A grand coalition of parties was formed for purposes of a government until unification. Only the PDS and *Bündnis 90* were not part of
this government. As early as 20 March, the government decided in
favour of economic and currency union on 1 July 1990. This was
confirmed as the agreed date at a meeting between Chancellor Kohl
and the new GDR prime minister de Maizière on 24 April. The newly
formed *Länder* of the GDR would join the Federal Republic on 3

October, and the first all-German elections were to be held on 2 December 1990.

The leaders of the four countries which had been Allies in World War II – Gorbachev of the Soviet Union, Mitterand of France, Thatcher of the UK and Bush of the USA – were equally overtaken by the momentum of events in the GDR. By the time they came together for the first time in Bonn on 5 May 1990 for talks with GDR and FRG leaders, they were aware that unification was totally unavoidable and that the timetable was now one of months. However, it was outside the Two Plus Four negotiations that the stumbling blocks to unification were removed, namely the question of united Germany's membership of NATO and, specifically, of the removal of Soviet troops from the territory of the GDR. These questions were resolved at a historic meeting between President Gorbachev and Chancellor Kohl in the Caucasus mountains on 16 July 1990. Gorbachev conceded the membership of NATO and agreed to the planned removal of Soviet troops. On 12 September 1990, the Two Plus Four negotiations were concluded in Moscow. This marked not just the formal end of the post-war period, but also the end of 'the terrible legacy of the First World War, and a century of totalitarianism' (James and Stone 1992: 9).

While the Two Plus Four negotiations were taking place, the FRG and GDR on 18 May signed a treaty setting 1 July as the implementation date for the currency, economic and social union of the two states, which was coupled with a large economic aid and reconstruction package for the GDR. The agreed union marked the actual disappearance of the GDR as a sovereign state, as its intra-border controls were also to cease on 1 July. For a few months there was a GDR as a state without any sovereignty criteria such as its own currency, its own economic planning, and its own border controls on its western border. On 22 July, the GDR parliament approved a bill re-establishing the *Länder* of Brandenburg, Mecklenburg-West Pomerania, Saxony, Thuringia and Saxony-Anhalt. On 23 August, a further bill providing for the GDR's accession to the Federal Republic with effect from 3 October was passed. It also ratified the agreement with the Federal Republic providing for an all-German general election on 2 December 1990. The Unification Treaty (*Einigungsvertrag*) was signed on 31 August. It was thereby agreed that, upon the GDR's accession to the Federal Republic, the *Länder* of the GDR would become *Länder* of the Federal Republic.

The GDR parliament met for the last time on 2 October 1990. On 3 October, a new Germany came into existence in the form of an enlarged Federal Republic of Germany. During this process, the leading role had been played by the Kohl government since the spring of 1990, but unification was of seminal historical significance in an international sense. In her introduction to an edited volume on unification, Marla Stone described unification as 'the last act of the post-war system and the first episode in an, as of now unnamed, post-cold war and post-Communist international order'. The shape of history had changed fundamentally: 'At the opening of the Berlin Wall, a bipolar world existed; by the declaration of a unified Germany, the former Soviet Union and Eastern bloc were desperately gazing westward for help and guidance' (James and Stone 1992: 18).

After March 1990, when the last GDR elections took place, the accession process happened at breath-taking speed. There is no doubt that Chancellor Kohl and his Foreign Minister Hans-Dietrich Genscher read the will of the GDR population for rapid unification correctly and managed to channel this momentum (see Kohl 1999). But they spurned the advice of opposition politicians, such as Oskar Lafontaine (SPD), and intellectuals, who favoured a lengthier process. It was felt for instance that unification via Article 146 of the Basic Law, which allowed for a new constitution decided on by the German people as a whole, would have been preferable to the route actually chosen, namely Article 23, which permitted the automatic application of the existing constitution to the new *Länder*. But the spirit of euphoria called for speed, and Article 23 was certainly the fastest route. The euphoria still prevailed on the day of the first all-German election since 1945 on 2 December 1990. Kohl and Genscher won these elections on the crest of a wave of popularity. The CDU/CSU gained 43.8 per cent of the vote, the FDP 11 per cent and the SPD 33.5 per cent. The CDU/CSU and FDP together held 398 of the 662 seats in the new *Bundestag*, and formed a coalition government.

For the SPD, the results were the worst since 1957. The Greens failed to win a single seat, but eight candidates of the East German *Bündnis 90* won seats in the upper house. They were the last political survivors of the intellectual opposition which had been so instrumental in triggering and propelling the *Wende*. A sour note for the political establishment of the Federal Republic was the fact that 17 candidates for the Party of Democratic Socialism also won seats. It was generally agreed, however, that within a few years the PDS would have disappeared in the process of the creation of 'inner unity'. But this process has proven longer than anticipated, and the PDS, far from having disappeared, remains the third strongest political force in the east (see Chapter 1).

6   Unification?

TERMINOLOGICAL DISUNITY

The already vast amount of literature on the unification of Germany reveals an often amorphous use of terminology, and disagreement as to periodization. The term *Wende* has been applied to the events of October and November 1989, but also to the whole period between January 1989 inside the GDR, when there were the first real signs of public dissidence, and March 1990, the month of the first free elections. The term is sometimes used by east Germans, moreover, as a point of temporal and spiritual orientation in a present in which they feel increasingly alienated, and there have been calls for a second *Wende* in which the hopes of the autumn 1989 revolution for a truly free and democratic society might be realized. The phase following the *Wende* is known as the accession phase (*Beitritt*), but while some date its beginning back to Kohl's November 1989 ten-point plan, others date this beginning to the March GDR elections, or to the coalition formed subsequently. Historically unique, the new parliament and government had as their objective their own dissolution and the dissolution of the state they represented. The term unification is usually used to refer to the official merging of the two states on 3 October 1990, but it has been pointed out that the various stages by which the GDR acceded to the Federal Republic – July 1990 currency union, ratification of the Unification Treaty, to name two examples – are themselves aspects of economic and fiscal unification, so that accession and unification can in a sense be seen as synonymous. Others have argued that unification started on 3 October 1990, but did not end there. If one conceives of unification as referring not just to the process of fiscal and political union, but also to issues of social, psychological and economic union, or issues of national identity, then it has certainly not come to end (hence the distinction between *external* and *internal* unification). The expression reunification, often used as a synonym, is certainly a misnomer. It implies that, in October 1990, two areas which had at one time in the past been made one through an act of union were now being united again, an historically inappropriate implication given that East and West Germany as they emerged after 1945 were, topographically and politically, quite new creations.

Terms such as accession and (re)unification are not the only ones used to refer to the events of 1990 and beyond. A typical satirical version of *Beitritt* is *Beitrott*, suggesting both a sheep-like and disenfranchised accession. In February 1990, the Governing Mayor of Berlin (West), Walter Momper, used the highly evocative term 'annexation' (*Anschluß*), hitherto associated with Austria's accession to the Third Reich in 1938 (cf. Rotfeld and Stützle 1991: 3). The implications of terms such as 'annexation' are clear: the east has been taken over by the west in a high-handed imperialist gesture. This idea recurs in references to the GDR as a 'colony' and to unification as 'colonization', as in German book-titles such as *Colony in One's Own Land* (Christ and Neubauer 1991) or *The Colonialization of the GDR* (Dümcke and Vilmar 1996). In the same vein, other German book-titles define the relationship between the old and new *Länder* as, essentially, one between capitalist exploiter and exploited. For example: *We are the Money: How the West Germans bought up the GDR* (Humann 1990), *The Lust for Property* (Luft 1996), or *Employer West, Employee East* (Hondrich, Joost, Koch-Arzberger and Wörndl 1993). In line with this theory of West German capitalist imperialism, it has even been suggested that the East German revolution was deliberately quashed in the interests of western greed (see *The Aborted Revolution* [Schneider 1990]).

German publications on the issue of unification have also focused on the issue of estrangement between east and west, an estrangement caused by 40 years of very separate histories under very different systems at the respective forefronts of opposing military blocs, and now reinforced by the east Germans' sense of being second-class citizens and the west Germans' irritation at what they perceive as east German ungratefulness. *Why we can't stand one another* runs the title of one publication (Ensel 1995), *German Alienation: the State of Consciousness in East and West* the title of another (Hardtwig and Winkler 1994). Not just historians, but psychoanalysts too have examined the issue of east–west differences, notably in *The Shock of Unity* (Mitscherlich and Runge 1993) and *Visiting our Brothers and Sisters* (Moser 1992). The conclusion of many commentators is that unification is as much a problem as a blessing. Hence titles such as *The Crisis of Unification* (Kocka 1995). The consensus is that it will – to borrow the sober title of another German publication – be a 'long path to unity' (Glaeßner 1993). This realization stands in stark contrast to the notion that unification was achieved on 3 October 1990 (for a comprehensive bibliography, see Abbey 1993).

ECONOMIC DISUNITY

Critics of the term unification claim that it presupposes a union of equals, which was not the case in 1990, where the GDR basically accepted terms of accession to the system of the Federal Republic. The GDR population was not given a chance to bring any influence to bear on the constitution, it was not given any share in the privatization of GDR industry – as originally envisaged by those who founded the idea of a Trust Holding Company for privatization – and few traces of the GDR's political, economic or educational system were taken over into the new Germany. Effectively, the west German system was simply extended eastwards. That this was simultaneously an act of dispossession is an argument for which there is powerful evidence. Many east Germans lived under threat of having the houses and flats they lived in, or the ground on which these stood, repossessed by former owners. In one extreme case, Franz zu Putbus claimed a sixth of the area of the Island of Rügen as his by right. The Trust Holding Company sold off the GDR's ailing industry to largely west German or foreign investors; only about a sixth went to east Germans. The east Germans, it is maintained, have been governed from the far-away west (Bonn), and by the west. The civil service was a largely west German import in terms of staff as well as structures. Thus in Brandenburg in 1991, 52 per cent of the higher-ranking civil servants came from the old *Länder*. In the important ministries in Brandenburg, this number was proportionately higher: the percentage of *Wessis* in the chancellery was 73 per cent, in the Ministry of Justice 72 per cent, and in the Ministry of Finance 67 per cent. The judiciary in the new *Länder* was largely west German, particularly in Berlin. The east Germans could do little to protect themselves against this influx, though humour helped: 'Foreigners, yes – Rhinelanders, no' (*Ausländer rein – Rheinländer raus!*) ran one east German joke. One firm even manufactured an 'anti-Wessi spray'.

Dispossession extended to mass job losses in both the public sector and in industry. The principle of cutting excess was given priority over job-sharing or part-time labour schemes, and over any principles of a gradualist transition from GDR to FRG structures which might have spread the impact, effects and extent of unemployment over a wider period and given people a realistic chance of acquiring new skills. In practice, the largely rigorous imposition of the western system meant that thousands of people literally fell into the considerable gaps created by the differences from the East German system or by the sudden superfluousness of some of its mirror-image institutions. One of the best examples of such 'gaps' is provided by the situation at primary and secondary schools. In the GDR, teachers taught more hours than their colleagues in the FRG, and class-sizes were smaller. Importing the west German system thus inevitably meant a reduction in teaching staff in the east. In some regions, about 40 per cent of teachers lost their jobs. By 1993, 140 schools in Thuringia had been closed. In 40 Thuringian schools, classes formerly taught separately had been bunched together; teaching hours were generally up by 50 per cent, and creche and school day-home facilities had been reduced. Higher education was also affected. Of the 3,000 to 4,000 university teachers and other academic staff who lost their jobs in Saxony-Anhalt, a considerable proportion were simply not needed any more because of the closing of the universities in Köthen, Leuna-Merseburg and Bernburg. In east Berlin, the loss of four universities meant that, by the middle of the 1990s, east Berlin enjoyed the dubious reputation of having the highest number of unemployed academics in the world.

In industry, the security of the GDR's system of permanent employment – maintained despite huge debts – gave way to severe rationalization in the name of capitalism. But need the unemployment have been so high? There was much criticism, not least from the then President of the Federal Bank Karl Otto Pöhl, of the July 1990 currency union. The sudden introduction of the strong West German *deutschmark* made East German industry uncompetitive overnight. Much criticism was levelled, moreover, at the Trust Holding Company for reckless privatization of firms. The original remit of the Company was for renovation (*Sanierung*) and privatization, not just the latter. The Unification Treaty also underlined the basic principle of regeneration and fair competition. In contravention of the fairness principle, west German firms bought up east German industry to kill potential competition and cream off investment subsidies. Promises to maintain certain levels of employment were frequently broken. Rather than revitalize industry bought from the Trust Fund, there was a tendency to sell off properties to the booming service industry, or use the industrial plant as an extended workbench for west German industry. Often, such 'extended workbenches' were the first to be shut down when economic problems hit. Complaints were made that capitalism in the east was not properly controlled by the state, and that there should have been wage subsidies to help ailing east German industry weather problems of low productivity and lack of market openings. Unemployment has been the scourge of the east, and has increased there steadily since 1990. There was a slight drop in the unemployment figures for the whole of Germany in 1998, but this drop only affected the west, where 116,000 fewer people were registered unemployed as compared with 1997 (leaving 2,904,000 without a job), while in the east there was an increase of 11,400 to 1,375,000 people unemployed. Besides, in December 1998 the unemployment figures rose again sharply from 10.2 per cent to 10.9 per cent. Once more, the east was particularly affected.

Even people with the good fortune to be employed in the east often feel like second-class citizens. Particular resentment was caused by the granting of so-called 'bush-money' to west Germans prepared to move their place of work from west to east. This term alone generated the feeling that west Germans were colonists, and east Germany little better than a Third World region. In Saxony-Anhalt, discussions as to whether Halle or Magdeburg should be made regional capital were decided in favour of Magdeburg, apparently, so rumour had it, because Magdeburg is nearer to west Germany, so that west Germans working there can get home quicker on the weekends. Generally, east Germans have to make do with lower wage levels than their colleagues in the west. By the end of 1997, wages within firms linked to the tariff system in the east had reached 89.2 per cent of those in the west. In the civil service, wage levels were 86.5 per cent of those in the west. Only in dynamic growth areas such as private banking was there east–west wage parity. Moreover, in the east, company employees often are graded in lower tariff groups than in the west, they do not enjoy the same additional benefits, and they work longer hours. Only about half of the employees in private industry are paid in accordance with the tariff system.

Within a few years of 3 October 1990, the east was being classed as a deindustrialized landscape. By the end of 1994, 97 out of 1,000 employees in the old *Länder* worked in industry, while in the new *Länder* the figure was as low as 43 out of 1000, compared with 130 3 years earlier (Luft 1996: 136). On the occasion of the Mecklenburg-West Pomerania FDP Party Congress in spring 1992, Rainer Ortleb, former FDP Federal Education Minister, pessimistically envisaged the possible development not of 'blossoming landscapes' in the east, as Kohl had predicted in March 1990, but of another kind of landscape, namely a 'huge nature reserve with a sausage stall'. Many east Germans were either unemployed, working in lower-paid jobs, or had moved to the west to find or take work. Not that they were always welcome. In 1996, inflammatory pamphlets were found near the east German town of Meiningen, not far from the former east–west border. The pamphlets claimed that east Germans had 'poured into the west like Huns when the border was opened, just to get their 100 marks welcome money'. East Germans were also accused of trying to take west German jobs away. The pamphlet added that it would not be difficult to find volunteers to re-erect the wall and even 'add another 10 metres to it'.

And yet this image of an unscrupulous west, not wanting to divide its spoils, not interested in helping to reconstruct the east, is in need of relativization. There have been cases of sincere investment in and commitment to the east. While there were indeed thousands of closures of traditional GDR industries and firms (Trabant, Robotron and Interflug are three main examples), some east German industry, notably Carl Zeiss in Jena, now run by former Minister-President of Baden-Wurttemberg Lothar Späth, has survived and even thrived, often with western support. Major banks made their way east – *Deutsche Bank* had 300 new branches there by the end of 1993, with some 12,500 employees. By December 1993, Daimler-Benz AG had invested 425 million marks in the east, Volkswagen 1.8 billion in manufacturing plants in Zwickau, Chemnitz and Eisenach, while Bayer AG invested 600 million in new branches in Bitterfeld.

Nor was the German government idle. The Trust Fund did become synonymous with rabid privatization, over two million job losses and massive deficits, partly due to mismanagement and being taken for a ride by western speculators (256 billion marks by 1995). But it must be remembered that the initial dividing up of the unwieldy, run-down and debt-ridden east German combines into some 12,000 private firms for selling off was a remarkable feat. As Trust Fund adviser André Leysen said: it is easy to make fish soup out of an aquarium, but harder to turn the soup back into an aquarium (Schirrmacher, Schiwy and Marsh 1995: 100). Moreover, the various models suggested as an alternative to privatization remain untested hypotheses. And, as time went on, Bonn did react to complaints that its priorities were wrong by setting up a *Management KG* to oversee the renovation of 75 east German firms (albeit with a mere 20,000 employees) prior to selling them. Massive sums of money have been pumped into a whole host of community projects and concessions to industry designed to promote east German infrastructures. By 1994, 160,705 million marks had been paid from the fund 'German Unity' to eastern regions and communities. The programme 'Upturn East' (*Gemeinschaftswerk Aufschwung Ost*), passed on 8 March 1991 by the *Bundestag* to help support investment and create jobs, was equipped with 12 billion marks in 1991 and again in 1992. Traffic, housing and the environment have been the repeated benefactors of support from Bonn.

East Germans tend to forget what the GDR was like. On 31 December 1989, 18 per cent of flats in the GDR had no bath or shower, while 24 per cent had no toilet, 53 per cent had no modern heating system, 84 per cent no telephone. Project *Telekom 2000*, launched soon after unification, aimed to increase the paltry 1.8 million phone connections in the former GDR to 7.5 million by 1997, the 22,000 pay and card phones to 70,000, and the 2,500 fax connections to 400,000. Five hundred thousand mobile telephone connections were to be installed, not to mention 5 million cable television connections – a novelty in the east. While the application of the term 'old burden' (*Altlast*) to the GDR is certainly in some sense defamatory, it is only too accurate as far as the environment is concerned. From the border eastwards – which was still infested with land-mines from the height of the Cold War – the landscape was anything from explosive to highly toxic. There were hosts of 'wild' rubbish dumps, in old mine-shafts for instance, containing rusty cars and toxic insecticides; poisonous substances had leaked into the groundwater, polluted rivers and lakes. Geriatric industrial plant churned out toxic waste. There was radioactive contamination due to uranium mining. Lignite mining had poisoned air, soil and water. In a lignite mining sanitation project for the Halle, Leipzig and Bitterfeld area, 32,000 jobs were created. Part of 'Upswing East' involved the creation of 400,000 temporary work placements (*ABMs*) in the east, 120,000 in environmental projects alone.

Pouring all this money into the east, however, was only partly successful in increasing industrial output. Nor could it overcome prejudice in the west towards east German products. Under the auspices of the government, 'Purchase Initiative East' (*Einkaufsinitiative Ost*) was inaugurated in 1994. The 87 firms who joined the initiative ordered 35 billion marks worth of goods and services from the east of the country. In August 1997, SPD and CDU called on their members to buy east German products such as Thuringer roasted sausages. Oskar Lafontaine expounded on how he looked forward in early summer to fresh asparagus from Brandenburg. By 1997, east German products had secured a mere 3 per cent of the west German, and only 20 per cent of the east

German market. In February 1997, leading west German supermarkets promised Kohl they would increase their supply of east German goods. In 1996 they ordered 14 per cent more than in 1995. At the end of June 1997, 50 'courageous entrepreneurs' from the east were conspicuously given awards by the Federation of German Industry in Munich. President Herzog gave a rousing speech describing it as 'a grand achievement of east German citizens' that they had overcome the collapse of the GDR system so 'constructively and innovatively'. Only 39 of these entrepreneurs were east German, and there was not one woman amongst them.

Some of these endeavours on the part of state and industry to help east German industry do smack of desperate, fig-leaf remedies in the face of western scepticism, monopolism and expansionism. The east was regarded as a massive and hungry market for western goods, not as a legitimate source of competition. Many western firms, moreover, have preferred to set up in Poland and Hungary, where wage and productivity costs are lower. Arguably, too, the west began to run out of patience with the east. The turning-point came with the approach of the Maastricht Treaty and European currency union. Finance Minister Waigel in 1996 and 1997 began to look for ways of saving money to meet the Maastricht criteria, and he targeted the 'Common Programme for Improving Regional Economic Structures' (GA), from which the east largely benefited. In September 1997, the regional economics ministers reluctantly agreed to cuts of 200 million marks in planned GA investment provision. In 1997 and 1998, there were discussions in Germany as to whether the system whereby the wealthier *Länder* help out the weaker *Länder* financially should be revised, and as to whether the system of German federalism should be modified in view of the fact that SPD-run *Länder* were blocking legislation on saving in the *Bundesrat*. In 1998, the CSU in the relatively rich Bavaria expressed irritation at having to support the east when many in the former GDR, instead of being grateful, preferred to vote PDS and long for the return of Honecker. These comments provoked anger in east Germany. In the face of rising crime and unemployment, the east has become increasingly sceptical about unification. A survey by Infratest Burke in January 1996 found out that only 33 per cent of east Germans prefer the FRG system in comparison with 51 per cent in 1990, while 22 per cent consider the GDR to be a better system in comparison with 11 per cent in 1990. While environmental problems had been the main anxiety of east Germans in 1990, fear of crime was the main one in 1996, with unemployment coming a close second, followed by fear of poverty.

Solutions

It remains to be seen whether the new SPD/Greens government will succeed in getting people back to work. In late 1998, the government started a programme called JUMP designed to lower unemployment among young people. One aspect of this programme is the encouragement of early retirement by promising full pension rights to people who retire at 60. But this will only work if firms are obliged to replace those who retire via this path with younger employees. The farce surrounding the recent ecological tax, which has been levied with disproportionate severity favouring large firms who use a lot of energy, does not augur well for the SPD's ability to curb the power of west German industry.

It also remains to be seen whether the formula that DM, free market and privatization automatically lead to success is viable in the current situation. The old Federal Republic's concept of a free social market economy presupposed and attempted to enhance fair competition. On unification, the east was economically and industrially in a parlous state. Its chances of asserting itself in the face of west German and world-wide competition were negligible. Arguably, not enough was done to create favourable preconditions in the east subsequent to unification. In the words of two German commentators, a seriously ill economy cannot win the 'game' against an export world champion; a mixed economy strategy based on a far-sighted framework on the part of the state should have been adopted (Priewe and Hickel 1991: 20).

It is has certainly not been prudent, as has often been the case, to interpret the post-unification crisis as a recession in the traditional economic sense. To date, no theory of economic cycles has allowed for the factor of the absorption of one economic system into another. Even the view that the enlarged Federal Republic, and specifically the five new *Länder*, would re-enact the economic processes which led to the West German economic miracle does not stand up to scrutiny, simply because a completely different set of economic, political, social, indeed global conditions applied post-1990 as applied in the 1950s (cf. Priewe and Hickel 1991: 224–228 and Schmidt 1993: 25f). Neither the five new *Länder*, nor for that matter any other former COMECON countries, are experiencing anything resembling a classical recession. Rather they are undergoing a transformation crisis in all spheres of life and in particular in the economic sphere. Even when violent recessions occurred in history, as in 1929, or for that matter in the immediate post-war years in the West, the structural and institutional aspects of the (capitalist) economy remained unchanged. Individual crises in the coal, steel, shipbuilding and other industries have never been in a comparable context, nor have they brought about the total collapse of one economic system and its replacement by another.

OSTALGIE

Comparisons can be tendentious, but they are also hard to resist. In the present climate of unemployment and rising crime rates in the east, it is understandable that many should long for precisely those elements of GDR society which, at the time, they had taken for granted: job security and security on the streets. That this security was the result of huge state debt and political repression generally does not enter the equation. It is understandable, given the feeling of political and social impotence generated by both unemployment and the east–west divide, that east Germans should look back wistfully at the *Wende*, when their protests led to the securing of elemental human rights such as freedom of movement and political participation. Understandable too is the tendency to equate capitalism with ruthless rationalization and greed, and to revalue the repressive GDR as a community of solidarity and sharing. In a sense, the success of the PDS is also the result of a redefinition. The PDS projects itself as the party which represents all that is good about democratic socialism, casting off its role as successor to the repressive SED. Indeed the PDS has succeeded in remodelling its image to such an extent that it now can get away with embodying those very principles and using those very slogans associated with the GDR opposition movement. Thus, during the Kosovo crisis in spring 1999, the PDS protested against NATO bombing under the motto 'Create Peace without Weapons'. Such is the irony of history.

If and when the employment and industrial situation in the east improves, this nostalgia for the GDR or the *Wende* may gradually dwindle. Most east Germans would not wish the GDR back as it existed; nor would they want to do without the benefits of capitalism, which, for some at least, has meant the chance of a greater freedom of choice. Nevertheless, even economic growth may not change the sense of division if the west is not prepared to abandon its position of exploiter, teacher, elder and better, and accept the viability of east German difference. Generally, such differences have been particularly vehemently rejected by the CDU. In Brandenburg's schools, children are not given obligatory teaching in Christian religion, but are taught 'Life formation, ethics and religion' (LER), which is not bound to a particular religion. The CDU has dismissed LER as a socialist-inspired atheistic attack on Christianity, but it can also be interpreted as an attempt to break with a long-standing Christian monopoly of religious education, while not being inherently anti-Christian. In 1997, the Erfurt Declaration was signed, a strongly east German document calling for greater political activity outside parliament, and for an end to the 'Cold War' against the social state. Because it advocated cooperation with the PDS, it was immediately discredited as but a disguised attempt to re-establish repressive socialism. Extra-parliamentary political movements have always had a hard time of it in the FRG, as have any ideas of putting social before economic values. The long battle in Brandenburg in the early 1990s surrounding the introduction of a constitution in which fundamental rights to a home and to a job were to be enshrined was a clear reflection of west German conservative opposition (notably by CDU constitutionalist Rupert Scholz) to any notion that industry and the state were to be bound into obligations of social justice. Only if this policy of rejecting all things eastern is modified will there be a serious prospect of east and west growing closer together.

7 Coming to terms with the past

After 1945, and again after 1990, Germany found itself faced with the task of coming to terms with the past. Between 1945 and 1990, but also to a degree subsequently, this past was the National Socialist one of dictatorship, war and genocide. Following the collapse of socialism in 1990, a 'second' past of dictatorship and injustice needed to be confronted. At the outset it must be stressed that the history of coming to terms with National Socialism was decisively shaped by the division of Germany and the divergent developments in East and West. Equally, the post-1990 attempt to overcome the legacy of socialism has been accompanied by embittered debates reflecting the continuation of a division between east and west in 'united' Germany.

THE ALLIES AND DENAZIFICATION

One Germany was responsible for National Socialism; two German states had to face its legacy. This fact alone meant that there would, inevitably, be two ways of approaching the problem. Initially, the manner of coming to terms with National Socialism was determined by the Allies. There was broad agreement among the Allies after the war that Germany should pay reparations for the war damage it inflicted, and compensation to the victims of Nazism; there was also broad agreement that leading Nazis should stand trial, and that Germany should be denazified, purging society of the ideological influence of Hitler. But as the Cold War intensified, the Western and Eastern Allies began to adapt their policies to the exigencies of politics. While the Russians exacted severe reparations from their zone, the western Allies took a more lenient line, especially as it became clear that an industrially weakened western Germany would be counterproductive in the contest with the Soviets. Denazification in the western zones was influenced by the practical need to get German society and bureaucracy up and running; thus the 'small' fish were dealt with first. The larger ones profited from the scaling down of denazification in 1948. In the Soviet zone, denazification became increasingly bound up with sovietization. Thus the Soviets interned not only (mostly small-scale) Nazis in the former concentration camps of Sachsenhausen and Buchenwald, but, as of 1946 onwards, Social Democrats and others perceived to be political opponents of the imposition of communism.

Both the Western Allies and the Soviets did put on trial and impose severe sentences on leading Nazis. Apart from those sentenced at the Nuremberg trials, the Western Allies levied some 5,000 sentences, 668 of them death sentences; in the Soviet zone, the number of sentences may have been as high as 20,000 by 1947 (436 of which were death sentences). But the moral credibility of the Allies was shaky, because of Hiroshima and Nagasaki on the American side, and because of the crimes of Stalinism on the Soviet side. Hence many Germans felt the various trials and other measures of denazification to be 'victors' justice'. When the Germans in the FRG and GDR took over the task of coming to terms with the past from their Allied overseers as of 1949, they administered it with a similar degree of moral self-righteousness, ambivalence and sense of political expediency. In this they were supported by their respective Allies.

WEST GERMANY AND THE NAZI PAST

Adenauer has been praised for his politics of conciliation towards Israel. On the basis of 1952 agreements which he pushed through against considerable political opposition within his own party, Adenauer paved the way for the payment of what amounted over the years to some 3.45 billion marks in compensation to Israel and the Jewish Claims Conference. The Federal Compensation Law of 1956 made it possible for individuals to apply for compensation to West Germany; by December 1985, about four-and-a-half million claims had been processed and over 60 billion marks paid out. But Adenauer's motive in encouraging compensation was largely political and as such almost exclusively West-oriented; he regarded it as one of the prices that had to be paid for the continuing integration of West Germany into European and trans-Atlantic structures. Thus a number of compensation agreements were signed with West European states, but not East European ones. Victims of Nazism living outside the former boundaries of the German Reich (1937) – and this largely affected Eastern European countries – had no right to apply for individual compensation. While Jews were compensated, victims without a political lobby and political relevance to West Germany, such as the Sinti and Roma, or homosexuals, largely went uncompensated.

That politics was Adenauer's main concern, not morality, became clear from his increasingly successful attempts in the 1950s to secure the release of prisoners sentenced by Allied courts, of prisoners-of-war, and to rehabilitate those who had been thrown out of the civil service in the course of denazification. The sympathy extended by the CDU towards the millions of refugees from the former eastern territories, moreover, was greater than that extended to victims of Nazism.

Putting a positive spin on Adenauer's 'politics of the past', it secured the cooperation and integration of German society, and the at least superficial acceptance of the new political order; but the creeping rehabilitation of former Nazis meant that West Germany laid itself open to accusations that it was a 'renazified' state. This policy of rehabilitation found its most drastic expression in the so-called 131 Law of 1951, which led to the reinstatement of former Nazi civil servants, and its most distasteful expression in Adenauer's employ of Hans Globke as state secretary (Globke had written an official commentary to the Nuremberg racial laws in 1935). It also was one of the reasons for the very slow, delayed and spasmodic judicial handling of Nazi crimes by West German courts.

Over time, however, things did change. The spirit of rebelliousness associated with 1968 was directed against what many young people felt to be the refusal of the older generation to face their responsibility for Nazism. It was also directed against the continuation of authoritarian elements in West German society. The 1968 generation undoubtedly painted too rosy a picture of the GDR. But this generation's support for the Marxist view, which held that capitalism was the essential force behind fascism, provided a necessary counterweight to the demonization of communism in West Germany. The integration of the FRG into anti-communist western alliances had made it all too easy for West Germans to argue that Hitler and the 'Wehrmacht' had been right to oppose bolshevism, and that the real menace had been and still was the Soviet Union. West Germany paid scrupulous attention to injustices in the GDR, assiduously gathering evidence of these at Salzgitter as of 1961. This was a way of putting moral pressure on the GDR, but also of diverting the focus away from the crimes of National Socialism.

The 1970s heralded a more open approach to issues of responsibility for Nazism. The Auschwitz trials of 1963 had done something to enhance awareness of the horrors of Nazism, but the greater impact was achieved by the showing of the American television series *Holocaust* in 1979. 1979 was also the year in which the Maidanek trials came to an end, and in which the Federal Parliament agreed to lift the statute of limitations on the prosecution of the crime of murder. This showed how far West Germany had travelled: all that had been possible in 1965 and 1969 was an extension of the period of possible prosecution. According to a 1979 survey, for the first time in the history of the FRG, a majority of people was in favour of continued prosecution of Nazi crimes – over 50 per cent as opposed to only 25 per cent in 1974 (Hoffmann 1992: 167–168).

A shift in generations, the passage of time, but also the advent of *ostpolitik* contributed to this greater openness; when Willi Brandt in 1970 fell to his knees before the Warsaw ghetto memorial in Poland, he did more for the acknowledgement of responsibility for Nazism in one moment than Adenauer had managed in years. The increasing political contact between West and East Germany in the 1970s and 1980s and the acceptance of the GDR into the international community resulted not just in a less strident anti-communist tone in West German politics; it also meant a reduction in the projection of moral blame onto the other side of the Wall, and, accordingly, a greater preparedness in the Federal Republic to confront the Nazi past. It was also under Brandt that concrete steps were taken to compensate East European victims of Nazism; thus in Geneva in November 1972, the FRG agreed to pay 100 million German marks to Polish victims of concentration camp experiments.

The change to a CDU-FDP coalition government under Chancellor Kohl in 1982 – the so-called 'intellectual and moral turning-point' – did result in attempts to relativize German guilt, not least in the Historians' Dispute of 1986, when historian Ernst Nolte characterized the holocaust as a response to the crimes of Stalinism. Nevertheless, the increasing spirit of openness prevailed through the 1980s. Compensation legislation was extended to allow provision for previously excluded victims, the Greens gave their support to a campaign for the rehabilitation of 'Wehrmacht' deserters, there was increasing interest in 'forgotten' victims such as Jehovah's Witnesses and homosexuals, youth work camps were set up at former concentration camps such as Neuengamme to secure traces of the past, and schoolchildren throughout Germany were encouraged by nationwide competitions to explore uncomfortable links between their native towns and Nazism.

EAST GERMANY AND THE NAZI PAST

The GDR never felt itself to be responsible for Nazism or for coming to terms with it. Many SED policitians at top level were, of course, communists who had either gone into exile when Hitler came to power, or had been incarcerated in concentration camps or prisons. There really was in the GDR a radical, if not absolute purge of those groups and professions which had been the backbone of the Nazi state. It was believed, moreover, that while the German people as a whole had succumbed to Nazism, the imposition of a socialist order in the GDR had opened the eyes of citizens to their previous mistakes and removed at one stroke all preconditions for a fascist revival. By contrast, it was stressed that these preconditions, namely capitalism and militarism, continued to obtain in the FRG which, unlike the GDR, had taken over bureaucrats and officials who had been active under Nazism. For 40 years, the GDR presented itself as liberated from fascism, and presented the FRG as its continuation both in spirit and in practice.

The GDR paid heavily in reparations, unlike West Germany. However, despite initial indications that it might, the GDR paid no compensation to Israel. Under the impact of the Cold War and of Soviet pro-Arab politics, Israel came to be regarded in the GDR as an imperialist force little different in its territorial politics to Hitler's Germany. Again and again, the SED argued that it was not prepared to 'support imperialism' by giving money to Israel. Anti-Zionism, which of course was also directed against the positive stance of the FRG towards Israel, was complemented by discrimination in the GDR itself. While Jews living in the GDR did receive a special pension as victims of fascism, they received less than those classified as anti-fascist resistance fighters. They were thus treated as 'second-class' victims. Following a wave of renewed anti-semitism in the 1950s after the Slansky trial in Czechoslovakia, many Jews left the GDR. Their numbers dwindled from 5,000 to between 300 and 400 by the end of the 1980s.

While West Germany was adjudged to have inherited Nazism, the GDR viewed itself as the heir to the tradition of the 'good' Germans who had resisted it. In a sense, the anti-fascist struggle was continuing, only now the Nazis were West Germans, Americans and Israelis, and the anti-fascist Allies were the East Germans and Soviets. To underpin this paradigm of historical inheritance and continuity, concentration camp memorial sites at Buchenwald and Sachsenhausen stressed the communist resistance in the camps and the importance of this ideological and spiritual legacy for the GDR, while pointing to examples of judicial leniency towards former SS leaders in West Germany. There was little room for the victims in this scheme of things. The fates of Jews, Sinti and non-communist groupings in the camps were severely underrepresented (Fulbrook 1999: 28–35).

Improved relations with West Germany did result in a softening of tone. Thus the new 1985 exhibition in Buchenwald dispensed largely with references to Nazi continuities in the Federal Republic. The 1980s also saw a certain attempt to commemorate the suffering of the Jews, particularly in 1988 to mark the 50th anniversary of the 'Night of Broken Glass' (the anti-semitic pogrom of 9–10 November 1938). There were various official events with Jewish representatives from West Germany and abroad. Free German Youth groups tidied up Jewish cemeteries, and local SED groups arranged ceremonies in synagogues. This very organized commemoration shows that propaganda was never far away. The state secretary for Church Matters Kurt Löffler stressed in a communiqué of 21 November that the 1988 commemoration had demonstrated the 'basic anti-fascist character of our socialist society' and shown that 'in socialism anti-semitism has been eliminated for ever' – a claim which ignored, for instance, the near-criminal neglect of Jewish cemeteries in East Berlin, notably that of the orthodox Jewish Community Adass Jisroel. In 1986 and again in 1988 the SED committed itself to rebuilding Berlin's most famous Jewish Synagogue and setting up a 'Centrum Judaicum'. Contacts were established to the University for Jewish Studies in Heidelberg, and to the World Jewish Council. There was even talk of readiness to pay compensation. But the collapse of the GDR meant that the socialist East Germany never had to renege on its policy of non-responsibility. Chancellor Kohl pressed forward with the original GDR plans to set up the Jewish Centre. It is often forgotten that this idea was not a West German one.

UNIFICATION AND THE PAST

With the end of the East–West conflict and the advent of unification, many of the mechanisms which had prevented an open confrontation with the Nazi past in East and West Germany also came to an end. Guilt, blame and responsibility could no longer be lobbed back and forth across the Berlin Wall. As a result, it could be centred within and upon the nation as a whole. This process of centring will soon be physically manifest when the Holocaust Memorial is built at the heart of Berlin. Another consequence of the end of the East–West conflict has been an opening up towards areas of the Nazi past which had been neglected or distorted because they did not accord with politically useful views of Nazism. The sufferings of the Jews are now fully documented at Buchenwald memorial site, while at Bergen-Belsen the history of the Wehrmacht-run POW camp for Russian soldiers is at last – after decades of silence – adequately represented. Gradually, the view of resistance, too communist-oriented in the East, too Stauffenberg-focused in the West, is becoming more rounded and differentiated. There is what might be termed a broadening of awareness of the extent of responsibility for Nazism. Goldhagen's (1996) book *Hitler's Willing Executioners* and the long-running 'Wehrmacht' exhibition shocked Germany into realizing that the 'ordinary soldier', indeed 'ordinary German', was not simply a helpless follower of Nazi orders. While those who lived through the Third Reich saw themselves subsequently as 'victims' of Hitler, today's Germans are openly confronting the issue of perpetration, notably in the reinclusion of the SS areas into concentration camp memorial sites at Sachsenhausen, Ravensbrück, Neuengamme and Dachau.

While this is all positive, what of the 'second' German past? In early 1990, the GDR itself began to seek ways of coming to terms with the injustices committed in the name of socialism: fugitives had been shot trying to cross the border to the West, political prisoners had languished and even been tortured in jails, the Stasi had spied on hundreds of thousands of people and ruined many lives and careers, while the SED had repressed and bullied an entire state. United Germany took over the task of redress as of October 1990. Over the last 10 years, there have been trials of those suspected of having committed crimes against humanity in the GDR. On the social side, there has been a purge of former GDR citizens with politically and morally tainted biographies within the civil service, the judiciary, the education system, and parliaments at communal, regional and federal level. This political and moral purge has often been accompanied by what one might term an ideological purge, particularly in the educational sector, where there is now no use for university lecturers versed in Marxist-Leninism, or for schoolteachers who have taught only subjects such as the anti-capitalist civic studies. The opening of the Stasi files under the control of the so-called 'Gauck Authority' has meant that the process of coming to terms has not rested entirely in the hands of the legislature, judiciary and administration. Former victims, as well as the media and researchers, are allowed varying degrees of access to the files. As a result, political, judicial and administrative processes often have been critically complemented by a degree of public control and involvement.

Without doubt united Germany has acted very swiftly in seeking to deal with the negative legacy of socialism. The mechanisms used have been the same as those used by West Germany in confronting the legacy of Nazism. In a sense, then, these mechanisms merely needed to be appropriated, adapted and reapplied. But this alone does not explain the speed. Germany has been at pains to demonstrate' that it does not intend to repeat the mistakes of the post-1945 period. It was Ralph Giordano who accused Germany – both the FRG and GDR – of being guilty on two counts: first for the crimes of Nazism, and second for not adequately facing these after 1945. His term 'the second guilt' became almost a household word (Giordano 1987). The speedy response to the crimes of socialism means that Germany cannot be accused of dilatoriness a second time. There is a more negative view of this swift response, however, one that is frequently expressed by former GDR citizens who now stand accused of crimes against humanity, but one which must be taken seriously nevertheless. On this view, the former West Germany wishes to demonstrate its moral superiority over the GDR by now, in a kind of cynical autopsy, pointing out all its failings and flaws. Indeed by revelling in a form of *Siegerjustiz* (victors' justice), west Germans seek to copy the judicial role of the Americans after 1945 and ally themselves with historical forces of progress.

DIFFERENTIATION

This view ignores the fact that, while it is indeed the west of the country that has driven the process of coming to terms with the GDR's legacy, it did not initiate it – that was the privilege of the GDR's reform movement. Moreover, the process is largely undertaken not on behalf of west Germans, but on behalf of east Germans who suffered under Honecker and Ulbricht and seek redress. It is true that, in the immediate post-unification years, the German authorities were on occasion too rigorous, but there has been a learning process. Vetting committees responsible for screening former GDR employees in the civil service came, in time, to understand that what mattered was not *which* functions these employees had had in the GDR, but *how* they had fulfilled them. Even the fact that an employee had collaborated with the Stasi was not automatically taken as a sign of unsuitability; committees sought to establish motives and conduct. Where committees were too rigorous, Labour and Administrative courts would, occasionally, overturn their decisions.

The spirit of increasing differentiation is borne out by statistics. On 18 January 1993, the authorities responsible for screening in secondary schools in Chemnitz reported in their final report that, between June 1991 and December 1992, 500 former honorary SED party secretaries, 358 school directors and 97 school inspectors had been dismissed. Yet the figures, which are typical, also reveal that 249 honorary party secretaries, 108 school directors and 14 school inspectors were able to continue working within the education sector. By 1996, 36,498 teachers had been screened for Stasi activities in Saxony-Anhalt; of the 887 who were found to have collaborated with the Stasi, only 133 were dismissed. According to the Ministry of the Interior in Mecklenburg-West Pomerania in a statistic ending on 31 December 1997, the screening of the whole regional public sector (80,577 people) had resulted in the discovery that 4,944 people had been involved with the Stasi; of these, only 1,215 people were dismissed. In view of such figures, it is inaccurate to talk of a 'witchhunt' or of victors' justice. Nor have authorities become increasingly 'lax': they have rather learnt to examine each case individually, a very laudable approach indeed.

The judicial coming to terms with the legacy of the GDR is characterized by a similar process of differentiation. One example will have to suffice here. The first border-guard trial, which began in late 1991, focused on the serious issue of the GDR's killings of fugitives at the German–German border. The verdict, pronounced on 20 January 1992, was manslaughter, and Ingo Heinrich, the guard considered guilty of firing the shots which killed Chris Gueffroy on 5 February 1989 was given a three-and-a-half year prison sentence. The presiding judge accused Heinrich of well-nigh executing Gueffroy; but on 25 March 1993, the Federal Court of Appeal ruled that the sentence was too harsh, among other things because Heinrich was 'in a certain sense the victim of the border regime', and also because Heinrich should not be made to, as it were, do penance for the fact that the small fish were up in court while the bigger ones were not. On 14 March 1994, the case having been referred back to the Berlin Regional Court, Heinrich's sentence was changed to a 2-year suspended sentence. The courts have subsequently levied mild suspended sentences on border-guards, except in cases of excessive killings, and gradually caught up with the bigger fish, on whom harder sentences have been imposed; thus, in 1993, Defence Minister Heinz Keßler was given a seven-and-a-half years prison sentence for his part in setting up the murderous regime at the border. On 25 August 1997, former GDR politicians Egon Krenz (6½ years) and Günter Schabowski (3 years) were sentenced for their part in condoning the border regime.

PROBLEMS AND INCONSISTENCIES

There are, however, a number of reasons to be dissatisfied with Germany's approach to the legacy of socialism. While compensation legislation for victims of Stalinism is now in place, it is awkward, unwieldy, impossibly bureaucratic and mean in the extreme. The reluctance of German industry and the German government to compensate adequately the surviving forced labourers from the Nazi period is a similar problem. Where money is required, coming to terms with the past tends to suffer. In the case of returning property to east Germans who were deprived of their homes when they fled to the west, Kohl's government soon discovered that the cheapest way to finance the righting of wrongs was to ask the former victims to pay. The principle of restitution before compensation was modified so that those who had a right to restitution had to pay a certain sum for the return of their own properties. Generally speaking, there has not been enough financial support from central government or the regions for the various institutions – such as the Gauck Authority and the Central Investigative Bureau for SED and Unification Criminality (ZERV) – responsible for dealing with various aspects of the GDR's criminal legacy.

A second, more serious problem is the lop-sidedness of the process of coming to terms with the 1945–1990 period. No-one can deny that the GDR has a miserable record in human rights. But the old West Germany was also not without its faults, not least the notorious *Berufsverbot* (the exclusion of communists from public employ) and, in the 1950s, the judicial persecution of West German communists and others who had links with the SED or even the Free German Youth. Yet no attempt has been made to confront these injustices; the then Minister of Justice Klaus Kinkel refused requests in this direction in 1992 and 1993. Moreover, what of West Germany's collaboration with the GDR? To what extent were the governments of Schmidt and Kohl responsible for morally and financially shoring up an inhuman system? Did the purchase of fugitives from GDR prisons not encourage the SED to incarcerate even more people? It does indeed seem as if all the blame for the problems and reactions of the Cold War is being placed on the GDR.

Whenever investigations into the GDR threatened to reveal West German complicity or involvement in dubious practices, the CDU showed no readiness to be self-critical. This was particularly the case with the Schalck-Golodkowski Investigative Committee in Bonn. In the course of the Committee's meetings in the early 1990s, it emerged that the CDU, CSU and West German industry, in violation of existing trade restriction agreements, may have supported Schalck-Golodkowski in his shady and frequently illegal procurement of hard currency and technology for the GDR. It also emerged that West German Minister of the Interior Wolfgang Schäuble, in cahoots with the Federal Intelligence Agency, may have offered Schalck some degree of protection after his flight from the GDR and possible prosecution there in December 1989. But the CDU blocked the Committee's attemps to firm up its suspicions, and the final official report severely played down any impression of industrial or political collusion. It was countered by Green Party parliamentarian Ingrid Köppe's alternative report, which sought to ruthlessly expose this collusion. In an act of censorship worthy of the former GDR, the CDU government slapped a 30-year publication ban on Köppe's report (but could not stop it circulating like some kind of *samisdat* journal). There are, then, two pasts: someone's else's and one's own. The former needs dealing with, the latter protecting.

This imbalance needs redressing. Perhaps it is in the course of being redressed. Certainly it is not without a certain ironic justice that the CDU, since December 1999, has been reeling under allegations of money laundering and slush funds. Undeclared donations, it seems, may even have influenced the purchase of the former GDR firm Leuna by the French firm Elf-Aquitaine. The fear that CDU decisions and even policies may have been 'bought' is yet to be dispelled. The CDU has forced Kohl to stand down as honorary party chairman; Kohl refused to name the donors of the funds in question. But this measure has not stemmed the flood of revelations and accusations. Some political commentators even predict the collapse of the CDU under the weight of scandal. The Northrhine-Westfalia SPD also stands accused of dubious practices: did current Federal President Johannes Rau declare private flights as business trips? If the nexus between repressive ideology and politics was a fault of the SED, the nexus between capital, industry and politics appears to be a fault of West Germany's leading parties.

8 Germany into the new millennium

In Chapter 1, it was argued that those East Germans who took to the streets in 1989 may be the truly revolutionary Germans. In Chapters 5, 6 and 7, it emerged that west Germany has been the controlling force, in political, economic and moral terms, in united Germany. This imbalance is one of the main sources of the lack of inner unity in Germany today. While few people doubt the need to apply standards of the western rule of law and established democratic practices to the east of the country, or the necessity of adapting the east to the realities of the capitalist world market, these standards and necessities have often been implemented with a degree of self-righteousness. It is to be hoped that the increasing awareness in Germany of the mistakes made in the transfer of capitalism in the east, and of the need for differentiation in assessing the past both in east and west, will prepare the way for a more interested and open-minded response to the east. This may, in turn, trigger a review of western paradigms in line with the more positive aspects of the east German legacy. What if it were the case that the west has the formal democratic standards, but those east Germans who were instrumental in bringing about change in 1989 the fresher democratic sense needed to help with a revitalization and a more judicious assertion of these standards? There is sometimes reason to suspect the west of instrumentalizing democratic mechanisms for undemocratic ends. In Erfurt, the GDR Church's opposition movement 'Open Work' (*Offene Arbeit*) survived the *Wende* and continues today, focusing not on SED repression, but on issues such as social injustice and unemployment under capitalism. The response of the Thuringian Office for the Protection of the Constitution, run largely by west Germans, was to put the group under observation in 1997. In this instance, east German experience was pitted against the conflation of political and industrial interests, a conflation which west German citizens often passively accept (as was evidenced by the lack of real protest against the SPD's recent decision to exempt larger industries from the ecological tax).

Normalization, a word which has a rather prosaic ring in English, is a favourite word of the Germans who, in the light of their turbulent, destructive and self-destructive history, wish for nothing else if not to be normal. Arguably, much has been done to achieve this normality. The fact that Germans now live under one political roof after the imposition of division after 1945 is certainly a facet of normalization. Peter Pulzer argues that the new Germany is the first true nation-state in German history, and in that sense unification has achieved the German quest for normality (Pulzer 1996: 303). That the Germans are likely to be content living under this roof, and not go out in search of a bigger one, seems certain. It also seems certain that the Germans will stay firmly locked within, indeed be exemplary in their loyalty to, EU and NATO structures. In this sense too, then, because the German *Sonderweg* (particular path) with its connotations of the exceptional and peculiar has come to an end, it would be valid to talk of normality.

The historian Hagen Schulze dismisses fears of renascent German nationalism for four reasons. First, the new shape of Germany is the only possible shape; there is no other legitimate alternative, especially not in the minds of its citizens. Second, for the first time in their history, the Germans can enjoy both freedom and unity. This is underlined by the all-powerful and accepted foundation provided by the Basic Law. Third, also for the first time in their history, the Germans have established a unified state not against the will of their neighbours, but with their consent. And, fourth, the new Germany is part of the west (Schulze 1996: 263–265). Another German historian, Jürgen Kocka, concurs with this view. For him, 1990 marked the end of Germany's historical 'particular path' and the confirmation of Germany's belonging to the west with its political, cultural, and societal values (Kocka 1995: 32).

Michael Salewski also sees the unification date of 3 October 1990 as the definitive solution of the 'German question', arguing that the struggle for Germany's place in Europe, which lasted at least 300 years, has come to an end (Salewski 1993: vol. 2, 428). Heinrich August Winkler sees unified Germany as a 'post-classic' nation state which has relinquished certain attributes of a sovereign state as a result of the mechanics of division and unification. Thus Germany relinquished aspects of military sovereignty; all its troops are part of NATO, i.e. it has no military powers of decision outside NATO, nor can it have atomic weapons. Economically it is bound into the European Union. These, of course, were the *conditiones sine qua non* of the formation of the old Federal Republic between 1949 and 1955, and were the underlying assumptions of the negotiations in 1990. Winkler argues that a new German 'particular road' away from western democracy is therefore unlikely.

Historians, however, show concern at the lack of inner unity within Germany and argue for more give and take. Kocka contends that the new Germany cannot be a mere continuation of the old Federal Republic, whatever the more dominant and powerful traditions (Kocka 1995: 43). This line of argument is taken up by another eminent German historian, Imanuel Geiss, who asks how the Germans 'will adapt to each other and cope with the far-reaching consequences of unification' (Geiss 1997: 105). Schulze talks of the need for an 'inner foundation' (*innere Gründung*) to the nation which will develop only if Germans are patient and if there is a national sense of solidarity (Schulze 1996: 265), while Winkler postulates that the Germans must still learn to be a nation if the inner unification process is to be successful (Hardtwig and Winkler 1994: 266). Much will depend, according to Stuart Parkes, on the success of the German economic model: 'if a sense of success and well-being develops in the former GDR as it did in the Federal Republic, then identification with the political system is likely to follow' (Parkes 1997: 55). It is interesting to note that Parkes uses a question mark at the end of his Chapter 4 heading 'The German Economy: the End of the "Miracle"?' He of course refers to the West German economic miracle, which is under threat. Also under threat is the 'social' of Germany's free social market economy and the system of wage bargaining.

The view that inner unity is a problem but outer unity assured, given Germany's firm commitment to multilateral western organizations, needs perhaps to be augmented by the awareness that the very western nature of Germany's orientation may be one of the causes of internal disunity. Correspondingly, the move by the German government and parliament from Bonn to Berlin in 1999 may represent an answer. As long as Germany was governed from Bonn, the attention of politicians was directed westwards over the Rhine, towards France and America; and it remained focused despite all eastward flows of cash on the old *Länder*, their problems and concerns. The move to Berlin will focus attention more on eastern European countries, and on the reality of continued division represented by Berlin. Nowhere is the east–west divide more palpable than here. The presence of the government in Berlin will, moreover, give east Germans the feeling that they are much more in the centre of political life than they were before, and that a new, more balanced and centred Republic has been born. The move symbolizes the end of the old FRG. The GDR came to an end shortly after its 40th birthday celebrations, the FRG in its 'Bonn Republic' form during the 50th birthday celebrations in 1999. What will take its place? In contrast to its association with past and present division, Berlin was historically the scene of solidarity, as during the 1948 Berlin Airlift, and, most memorably, in the scenes of jubilant celebrations and dancing on the Wall in November 1989, when the Germans truly seemed to feel and act as one. It is to be hoped that solidarity will also be the goal of the new Republic.

But not everyone sees Berlin so positively, given that the city can also be associated with the excesses of centralism and nationalism. The German parliament in 1991 voted by 337 to 320 to move to Berlin, the narrowest of margins. Those who opposed the move were concerned about the astronomical costs involved, or about mass unemployment in Bonn and the collapse of the town's infrastructure. Others simply saw no reason for moving. Minister of Employment Norbert Blüm protested at 'collective resettlement' and opined that nations should not carry their homes around with them like snails. The main worry, however, was that moving to Berlin might endanger federalism, liberal values and 'grown' democracy (*gewachsene Demokratie*), as if these characteristics somehow emanated from the walls of Bonn's architecture, while something altogether more ominous would seep from those of Berlin. Perhaps the frenetic rebuilding programme in Berlin represents a desperate attempt to construct a historically less tainted environment, while building a Holocaust Memorial on the site of the former Reich Ministries' Gardens or Goebbels's bunker might be interpreted on one level as a profoundly symbolic attempt to lay the ghost of the past.

All in all, Berlin holds more promise than it represents threat. It is worth recalling that, when the vote was taken in 1991, east German politicians largely backed Berlin. The PDS voted in favour, as did east Germans such as Konrad Weiß (*Bündnis 90/Die Grünen*), who claimed at the time that Bonn was for people who had everything behind them, and that it was the capital of the old Federal Republic, which was as 'dead as the GDR'. The spectre of nationalism conjured up by some Bonn-supporting politicians was, one suspects, designed to ward off the other spectre of a more eastward-oriented republic, which is what lies in the interests of the east Germans. During the recent Kosovo crisis, the Germans supported NATO air-strikes, and much attention was paid in the press in Germany (and Serbia) to the fact that here were Germans, for the first time since 1945, getting involved in a war in a country they had already attacked in 1941 – under the auspices of a Green Foreign Minister, whose party was supposedly pacifist. But against this must be set the fact of Germany's insistence on looking for a political rather than a military solution, and its stern resistance to ground-troops (hence Schröder was a 'dove', Blair a 'hawk'). There was an awareness of Germany's proximity to the former Yugoslavia, a wish to mediate and find an acceptable compromise. The German government's role as mediator between 'west' and 'east' internationally became increasingly pronounced the nearer the move to Berlin came. The move to Berlin may also precipitate its role as mediator within its own people.

Bibliography

Those works and articles in English particularly recommended for further reading are marked with an asterisk.

*Abbey, W. (ed.) (1993) *Two Into One: Germany 1989–1992: A Bibliography of the 'Wende'*, London: University of London Institute of Germanic Studies.

Akademie der Wissenschaften der UdSSR (ed.) (1955) *Politische Ökonomie: Lehrbuch*, Berlin: Institut für Ökonomie.

Bahro, R. (1977) *Die Alternative*, Frankfurt am Main: EVA.

—— (1979) 'Selbstinterview', in R. Bahro, *Ich werde meinen Weg fortsetzen. Eine Dokumentation*, Frankfurt am Main: EVA, 56–73.

—— (1980) Mandel, E. and von Oertzen, P. *Was da alles auf uns zukommt... Perspektiven der 80er Jahre*, Berlin: Olle and Wolter.

*Baring, A. (ed.) (1994) *Germany's New Position in Europe*, Oxford: Berg.

Bender, P. (1998a) 'Vereinigen können sich nur Gleiche: Über die dreifache Enteignung der Ostdeutschen', *Merkur* 12,52: 73–79.

—— (1998b) 'Anfang und Ende des Kalten Krieges: Die Berlinkrisen und ihre Folgen', *Merkur* 12,52: 1143–1154.

Biefang, A. (1995) 'Die Wiederentstehung politischer Parteien in Deutschland nach 1945', *Aus Politik und Zeitgeschichte: Beilage zur Wochenzeitung Das Parlament* B 18–19/95: 34–46.

Bodensieck, H. (ed.) (1972) *Die deutsche Frage seit dem Zweiten Weltkrieg*, Stuttgart: Klett.

Boßmann, D. (ed.) (1978) *Schüler über die Einheit der Nation*, Frankfurt am Main: Fischer.

*Cecil, R. (1971) 'Germany and Reunification', in J. P. Payne (ed.) *Germany Today*, London: Macmillan, 1–27.

*Childs, D. (1983) *The GDR, Moscow's German Ally*, London: Allen and Unwin.

Christ, P. and Neubauer, R. (1991) *Kolonie im eigenen Land: Die Treuhand, Bonn und die Wirtschaftskatastrophe der fünf neuen Länder*, Berlin: Rowohlt.

Claeys, G. (1980) 'Bahro's *Alternative*', *Radical Philosophy* 25: 27–30.

Cohen, G. A. (1981) *Karl Marx's Theory of History: A Defence*, Princeton: Princeton University Press.

Dahn, D. (1997) *Westwärts und nicht vergessen: Vom Unbehagen in der Einheit*, Reinbek bei Hamburg: Rowohlt.

*Deighton, A. (1990) *The Impossible Peace: Britain, the Division of Germany and the Origins of the Cold War*, Oxford: Oxford University Press.

Dümcke, W. and Vilmar, F. (eds) (1996) *Kolonialisierung der DDR: Kritische Analysen und Alternativen des Einigungsprozesses*, Münster: agenda.

*Dyson, K. (1996) 'The Economic Order – Still Modell Deutschland?', in G. Smith, W. E. Paterson and S. Padgett (eds), *Developments in German Politics 2*, Basingstoke: Macmillan, 194–210.

Ensel, L. (1995) *Warum wir uns nicht leiden mögen. Was Ossis und Wessis voneinander halten*, Münster: agenda.

*Evans, R. (1996) *Rereading German History 1800–1996: From Unification to Reunification*, London: Routledge.

Farquharson, J. (1985) *The Western Allies and the Politics of Food*, Leamington Spa: Berg.

—— (1988) 'Land Reform in the British Zone, 1945–1947', *German History* 6/88: 35–36.

FDGB (ed.) (1987) *Protokoll des 11. FDGB-Kongresses vom 22. bis 25. April 1987*, Berlin: FDGB.

*Fogg, D. (1984) 'Exodus from a Promised Land: The Biermann Affair', in I. Wallace (ed.) *The Writer and Society in the GDR*, Tayport: Hutton Press, 134–51.

Fricke, K.-W. (1964) *Selbstbehauptung und Widerstand in der Sowjetischen Besatzungszone Deutschlands*, Bonn and Berlin: Bundesministerium für Gesamtdeutsche Fragen.

*Fulbrook, M. (1991) *The Fontana History of Germany 1918–1990: The Divided Nation*, London: Fontana.

—— (1995) *Anatomy of a Dictatorship: Inside the GDR 1949–1989*, Oxford: Oxford University Press.

—— (1999) *German National Identity after the Holocaust*, Oxford: Polity Press.

Füssl, K.-H. (1995) 'Restauration und Neubeginn: Gesellschaftliche, kulturelle und reformpädagogische Ziele der amerikanischen "Re-education" - Politik nach 1945', *Aus Politik und Zeitgeschichte: Beilage zur Wochenzeitung Das Parlament* B 18–19/95: 3–14.

*Garton Ash, T. (1993) *In Europe's Name: Germany and the Divided Continent*, London: Jonathan Cape.

*Geiss, I. (1997) *The Question of Unification 1806–1990*, London and New York: Routledge.

Giordano, Ralph (1987) *Die zweite Schuld oder Von der Last Deutscher zu sein*, Hamburg: Rasch und Röhring.

Glaeßner, G.-J. (ed.) (1993) *Der lange Weg zur Einheit*, Berlin: Dietz.

*Glaeßner, G.-J. and Wallace, I. (eds) (1992) *The German Revolution of 1989: Causes and Consequences*, Oxford: Berg.

Glaser, H. (ed.) (1999) *Die Mauer fiel, die Mauer steht: Ein deutsches Lesebuch 1989-1999*, Munich: DTV.

*Glees, A. (1996) *Reinventing Germany: German Political Developments since 1945*, Oxford and Washington: Berg.

Goldhagen, D.J. (1996) *Hitler's Willing Executioners*, London: Little, Brown.

*Gorbachev, M. (1996) *Memoirs*, London: Doubleday.

Grosser, A. (1974) *Geschichte Deutschlands seit 1945*, Munich: DTV.

Habermas, J. (1995) *Die Normalität einer Berliner Republik*, Frankfurt am Main: Suhrkamp.

Hardtwig, W. and Winkler, H. A. (eds) (1994) *Deutsche Entfremdung: Zum Befinden in Ost und West*, Munich: C. H. Beck.

*Herf, J. (1997) *Divided Memory: The Nazi Past in the Two Germanys*, Cambridge, Massachusetts: Harvard University Press.

Hettlage, R. and Lenz, K. (eds) (1995) *Deutschland nach der Wende*, Munich: C. H. Beck.

Hoffman, C. (1992) *Stunden Null? Vergangenheitsbewältigung in Deutschland 1945 und 1989*, Bonn: Bouvier.

Hondrich, K. O., Joost, A., Koch-Arzberger, C. and Wörndl, B. (1993) *Arbeitgeber West-Arbeitnehmer Ost*, Berlin: Aufbau.

Honecker, H. (1984) *Entwickelter Sozialismus und Gewerkschaften*, Berlin: Verlag Tribüne.

Humann, K. (ed.) (1990) *Wir sind das Geld: Wie die Westdeutschen die DDR aufkaufen*, Reinbek bei Hamburg: Rowohlt.

IFM (1987) *Grenzfall*, Berlin: Initiative für Frieden und Menschenrechte.

*James, H. and Stone, M. (eds) (1992) *When the Wall Came Down: Reactions to German Unification*, New York and London: Routledge.

Janßen, K.-H. (1996) 'Der Vertrag, der keiner war', *Die Zeit* 11: 12.

Jarausch, K. H. (1998) 'Realer Sozialismus als Fürsorgediktatur: Zur begrifflichen Einordnung der DDR', *Aus Politik und Zeitgeschichte: Beilage zur Wochenzeitung Das Parlament* B 20/98: 33–46

*Jarausch, K. H. and Gransow, V. (1994) *Uniting Germany: Documents and Debates 1944–1993*, Providence and Oxford: Berghahn.

Johnson, J. and Childs, J. (1981) *West German Politics and Society*, London: Croom Helm.

Jung, O. (1992) 'Kein Volksentscheid im Kalten Krieg: Zum Konzept einer plebiszitären Quarantäne für die junge Bundesrepublik 1948/49', *Aus Politik und Zeitgeschichte: Beilage zur Wochenzeitung Das Parlament* B 45/92: 16–30

Jürgensen, K. (1997) 'Die britische Besatzungspolitik 1945–1949', *Aus Politik und Zeitgeschichte: Beilage zur Wochenzeitung Das Parlament* B 6/97: 15–29.

Keiderling, G. (1998) *Rosinenbomber über Berlin: Währungsreform, Blockade, Luftbrücke, Teilung*, Berlin: Dietz.

Kleinert, C., Krüger, W. and Williams, H. (1998) 'Einstellungen junger Deutscher gegenüber ausländischen Mitbürgern und ihre Bedeutung hinsichtlich politischer Orientierungen. Ausgewählte Ergebnisse des DJI-

Jugendsurvey 1997', *Aus Politik und Zeitgeschichte: Beilage zur Wochenzeitung Das Parlament* B 31/98: 14–27.

Kocka, J. (1995) *Vereinigungskrise*, Göttingen: Vandenhoeck & Ruprecht.

Kohl, H. (1999) *Ich wollte Deutschlands Einheit*, Berlin and Frankfurt am Main: Ullstein.

Koop, V. (1998) *Kein Kampf um Berlin? Deutsche Politik zur Zeit der Berlin-Blockade 1948/1949*, Bonn: Bouvier.

*Krisch, H. (1985) *The German Democratic Republic, The Search for Identity*, Boulder, Colorado: Westview Press.

Kuhrt, E., Buck, H. F. and Holzweibig, G. (eds) (1996) *Am Ende des realen Sozialismus*, Opladen: Leske und Budrich.

Laitenberger, V. (1988) 'Auf dem Weg zur Währungs- und Wirtschaftsreform: Ludwig Erhards Wirtschaftspolitik im Frühjahr 1948', *Aus Politik und Zeitgeschichte: Beilage zur Wochenzeitung Das Parlament* B 23/88: 29–44.

*Lewis, D. and McKenzie, J. R. P. (eds) (1995) *The New Germany: Social, Political and Cultural Challenges of Unification*, Exeter: University of Exeter Press.

Loth, W. (1994) *Stalins ungeliebtes Kind: Warum Moskau die DDR nicht wollte*, Berlin: Rowohlt.

Luft, C. (1996) *Die Lust am Eigentum: Auf den Spuren der deutschen Treuhand*, Zurich: Orel Füssli.

Mai, G. (1988) 'Der Alliierte Kontrollrat in Deutschland 1945–1948: Von der geteilten Kontrolle zur kontrollierten Teilung', *Aus Politik und Zeitgeschichte: Beilage zur Wochenzeitung Das Parlament* B 23/88: 3-14.

*Mann, G. (1974) *The History of Germany since 1789*, Harmondsworth: Penguin.

Marcuse, H. (1978) 'Protosozialismus und Spätkapitalismus. Versuch einer revolutionstheoretischen Synthese von Bahros Ansatz', *Kritik* 6/XIX: 5–27.

*Marsh, D. (1994) *Germany and Europe, The Crisis of Unity*, London: Heinemann.

McCauley, M. (1981) 'Social Policy under Honecker', in I. Wallace (ed.) *The GDR under Honecker 1971–1981*, GDR Monitor Special Series No. 1, Dundee: Hutton Press, 3–20.

*—— (1983) *The German Democratic Republic since 1945*, London and Basingstoke: Macmillan.

McLennan, D. (ed.) *Marx's Grundrisse*, London, Toronto, Sydney and New York: Granada.

*Merkl, P. (ed.) (1995) *The Federal Republic of Germany at Forty Five*, Basingstoke: Macmillan.

Mitscherlich, M. and Runge, I. (1993) *Der Einheitsschock: Die Deutschen suchen eine neue Identität*, Hamburg: Klein.

Moser, T. (1992) *Besuche bei Brüdern und Schwestern*, Frankfurt am Main: Suhrkamp.

Neubert, E. (1997) *Geschichte der Opposition in der DDR 1949–1989*, Bonn: Bundeszentrale für Politische Bildung.

Niclauß, K.-H. (1992) 'Der Parlamentarische Rat und die plebiszitären Elemente', *Aus Politik und Zeitgeschichte: Beilage zur Wochenzeitung Das Parlament* B 45/92: 3–15.

Noelle, E. and Neumann, E. P. (1967) *The Germans: Public Opinion Polls 1947–1966*, Allensbach and Bonn: Verlag für Demoskopie.

Nolte, E. (1995) *Die Deutschen und ihre Vergangenheiten*, Frankfurt am Main: Propyläen.

*Parkes, S. (1997) *Understanding Contemporary Germany*, London and New York: Routledge.

*Pond, Elizabeth (1993) *Beyond the Wall, Germany's Road to Unification*, Washington: The Brookings Institute.

Poppe, U. (1995) 'Der Weg ist das Ziel: Zum Selbstverständnis und der politischen Rolle oppositioneller Gruppen der achtziger Jahre', in U. Poppe, R. Eckert and I. O. Kowalczuk (eds) *Zwischen Selbstbehauptung und Anpassung: Formen des Widerstandes und der Opposition in der DDR*, Berlin: Links, 244–272.

*Press and Information Office of the Government of the Federal Republic of Germany (ed.) (1972) *Facts about Germany*, Bonn: Presse- und Informationsamt.

Presse- und Informationsamt der Bundesregierung (ed.) (1994) *Deutschland: Von der Teilung zur Einheit*, Bonn: Presse- und Informationsamt.

Priewe, J. and Hickel, R. (1991) *Der Preis der Einheit*, Frankfurt am Main: Fischer.

*Pulzer, P. (1995) *German Politics 1945–95*, Oxford: Oxford University Press.

—— (1996) 'Model or Exception – Germany as a Normal State?', in G. Smith, W. E. Paterson and S. Padgett (eds) *Developments in German Politics 2*, Basingstoke and London: Macmillan, 303–316.

*Radice, G. (1995) *The New Germans*, London: Michael Joseph.

*Rotfeld, A. D. and Stützle, W. (eds) (1991) *Germany and Europe in Transition*, Oxford: Oxford University Press.

Ruhm von Oppen, B. (ed.) (1955) *Documents on Germany under Occupation 1945–1954*, London, New York and Toronto: Granada.

Rutschky, M. (1995) 'Wie erst jetzt die DDR entsteht', *Merkur* 49/95: 851–864.

Ryder, A. J. (1973) *Twentieth Century Germany: From Bismarck to Brandt*, Basingstoke: Macmillan.

Salewski, M. (1993) *Deutschland: eine politische Geschichte*, 2 vols., Munich: C. H. Beck.

Schirrmacher, F., Schiwy, P. and Marsh, D. (1995) *Die Neue Republik*, Berlin: Rowohlt.

Schlupp, F. (1980) 'Modell Deutschland and the International Division of Labour', in E. Krippendorff and V. Rittberger (eds) *The Foreign Policy of West Germany*, London and Beverly Hills: Sage Publications, 33–100.

Schmidt, H. (1993) *Handeln für Deutschland*, Berlin: Rowohlt.

Schneider, M. (1990) *Die abgetriebene Revolution: Von der Staatsfirma in die DDR-Kolonie*, Berlin: Elefanten Press.

Schulze, H. (1996) *Kleine Deutsche Geschichte*, Munich: C. H. Beck.

—— (1997) *Der Weg zum Nationalstaat*, Munich: DTV.

Sharp, T. (1975) *The Wartime Alliance and the Zonal Division of Germany*, Oxford: Clarendon Press.

Smith, G., Paterson, W. E. and Padgett, S. (eds) (1996) *Developments in German Politics 2*, Basingstoke: Macmillan.

Steele, J. (1977) *Socialism with a German Face*, London: Macmillan.

Steininger, R. (1983) *Deutsche Geschichte 1945–1961: Darstellung und Dokumente in zwei Bänden*, Frankfurt am Main: Fischer.

The Panorama DDR (ed.) (1986) *Five-Year-Plan-Act: The Development of the GDR's National Economy in the Period 1986–1990*, Dresden: Zeit im Bild.

Thomaneck, J. (1990) 'A Trade Union Movement of the New Type: The Third FDGB Congress', *GDR Monitor* 22: 31–43.

—— (1993) 'Anna Seghers and the Janka Trial: A Case Study in Intellectual Obfuscation', *German Life and Letters* 46: 156–161.

*Thurich, E. and Endlich, H. (1971) *Zweimal Deutschland: Lehrbuch für Politik und Zeitgeschichte*, Frankfurt am Main, Berlin and Munich: Moritz Diesterweg.

Warnke, H. (1977) 'Erfahrungen der Gewerkschaftsarbeit nach dem 8. FDGB-Kongreß bei der Verwirklichung der Hauptaufgabe', in *Gewerkschaften – Sachwalter der Arbeiterinteressen: Ausgewählte Reden und Aufsätze 1971–1975*, Berlin: Tribüne, 263–286.

*Watson, A. (1992) *The Germans: Who are they now?*, London: Methuen.

Weidenfeld, W. (1999) *Außenpolitik für die deutsche Einheit: Die Entscheidungsjahre 1989/90*, Stuttgart: DVA.

Wettig, G. (1998) book reviews of K.-R. Korte (1998) *Deutschlandpolitik in Helmut Kohls Kanzlerschaft*, Stuttgart: DVA, and H. J. Küsters and D. Hofmann (eds) (1998) *Deutsche Einheit*, Munich: Oldenbourg, *Außenpolitik: German Foreign Affairs Review* 49: 83–87.

*Wolle, S. (1998) *Die heile Welt der Diktatur: Alltag und Herrschaft in der DDR 1971–1989*, Berlin: Links.

*Woods, R. (1986) *Opposition in the GDR under Honecker, 1971–1985: An Introduction and Documentation*, Basingstoke: Macmillan.

*Woods Eisenberg, C. (1996) *Drawing the Line: The American Decision to divide Germany, 1944–1949*, Cambridge: Cambridge University Press.

Index

Ackermann, Anton 23
Adenauer, Konrad 14, 17, 22–3,
  32–3, 36–8, 43–4, 80–2
Afghanistan 45
Ahlen resolution 21
Allied Control Council 12–13, 38
Allied High Command 11
Arndt, Adolf 36
Arnold, Karl 21
Asylum seekers 1
Auschwitz trials 81
Austria 69

Bad Godesberg Programme 23
Baden 4
Baden-Wurttemberg 73
Bahro, Rudolf 47–9
Basic Treaty 44
Bavaria 4, 7–8, 13–14, 19
Belgium 33, 44
Bergen-Belsen 85
Berlin 1, 4, 8–9, 11, 60, 71, 84, 92–3
Berlin blockade 26, 34–5, 39, 93
Berlin crisis 42–3
Berlin Wall 39, 42–3, 46, 61, 63, 67,
  82, 84, 93
Berufsverbot 88
Biermann, Wolf 47
Blair, Tony 94
Blüm, Norbert 93
Bohley, Bärbel 62
Brandenburg 4, 9, 66, 70, 74, 77–8
Brandt, Willi 43, 82
Brasch, Peter 59
Braun, Volker 59

Bremen 2, 13–14
Britain 11–23, 32–7, 41, 44
Brown, Lewis 34
Bruyn, Günter de 59
Buchenwald 80, 83–5
Bündnis 65, 67
Bush, George 66
Byrnes, James 33

Ceaucescu, Nicolae 61
Central Committee (GDR) 30, 62
Central Investigative Bureau for
  SED and Unification Criminality
  (ZERV) 88
Centrum Judaicum 84
Chernobyl disaster 49
China 7, 61
Christian Democratic Union (CDU)
  1, 5, 7–9, 14, 21, 24, 26–7, 30, 33,
  36, 43–6, 65, 74, 77–8, 81–2, 89
Christian Social Union (CSU) 5, 9,
  36, 67, 75, 89
Churchill, Winston 11
Clay, Lucius 20, 34–5
Cold War 6, 15, 20, 31, 35–7, 41,
  45, 61, 67, 78–9, 82, 89
Communist Party of Germany
  (KPD) 14, 21
Communist Party of the Soviet
  Union (CPSU) 48, 57
Conference on Security and
  Cooperation in Europe (CSCE)
  51
Council for Mutual and Economic
  Assistance (COMECON) 76

Council of Europe 31
Croatia 7
Curzon line 12
Czech Republic 7, 16, 83

Dachau 85
Democracy Now 62
Democratic Awakening 65
Democratic Farmers' Party of
    Germany (DBD) 24, 26–7, 30
Democratic Womens' League 27, 29
Denazification 13, 79–80
Division (of Germany): Allied divi-
    sion of 11–29; bizonal economic
    administration 21–2; creation of
    Länder 13; currency reform 34,
    38; discourse of division 37–41;
    Economic Council and Executive
    Committee 15–16; emergence of
    East Germany 23–30; emergence
    of West Germany 15–23; issue of
    responsibility for 9, 12, 31–41;
    land reform, 24–5; role of consti-
    tution 27–8; self-determination
    35–7; separation of Germany into
    zones 11–15; West German policy
    of strength 36–8
Douglas, Sholto 38
Dulles, John 36

Eisenhower, Dwight 21
Environment Library 49, 58
Eppelmann, Rainer 50
Erfurt Declaration 78
Erhard, Ludwig 22, 41
European Atomic Energy
    Community 31
European Coal and Steel
    Community (ECSC) 31
European Economic Community
    (EEC) 37
European Union (EU) 7, 91

Farmers' Mutual Aid Association
    (VdgB) 25
Federal Republic of Germany
    (FRG): Basic Law 18–20, 35, 67,
    70, 91; coming to terms with the
    past 40–1, 79–82, 91; economic

miracle 11, 38–9, 76, 92; embassies
    in eastern bloc 62; foundation of
    15–23; integration into West 31;
    Modell Deutschland 40; relations
    with East Germany 31–41, 43–6;
    unification with GDR 1, 63–78
France 11–23, 32–7, 41, 44
Frankfurt Documents 17
Free Democratic Party (FDP) 8–9,
    14, 21, 24, 65, 67, 72, 82
Free German Trade Union (FDGB)
    26, 53–6
Free German Youth 25–7, 29, 58,
    84, 88
Frey, Gerhard 6

Gauck, Joachim 85, 88
Genscher, Hans-Dietrich 7, 62, 67
German Democratic Republic
    (GDR): banning of *Sputnik* 59,
    61; censorship 59–60; coming to
    terms with the past 10, 39–40,
    83–8; constitution 26–8, 53, 65;
    emergence of new parties 62; emi-
    gration to the West 42–3; factors
    in gradual collapse 42–56; Five
    Year Plan 55; foundation of
    23–30; impact of *glasnost* 57–9;
    identity 3–4, 6; integration into
    East 31; new course 42; nostalgia
    for 4, 77–8; opposition movement
    47–52, 90; relations with West
    Germany 31–41, 43–6; revolution
    in 1989 4–5, 10, 46, 57–67; Round
    Table talks 65; trade unions 52–6;
    unification with FRG 1, 63–78;
    uprising in 1953 39–40, 43, 46
German People's Union (DVU) 5–7
German Social Union (DSU) 65
Giordano, Ralph 86
Globke, Hans 81
Goldhagen, Daniel 85
Gorbachev, Mikhail 57, 62–3, 66
Gramsci, Antonio, 48
Greens/B'90 7–9, 65, 67, 76, 82, 89,
    93–4
Grotewohl, Otto 26
Gueffroy, Chris 87

Hager, Kurt 57

Hallstein Doctrine 38, 41
Hamburg 11, 13–14
Hanover 19
Harich, Wolfgang 47
Harriman, Averell 34
Havemann, Robert 47, 50
Hein, Christoph 59–60
Heinrich, Ingo 87
Helsinki Conference 44, 49
Herzog, Roman 75
Hesse 7, 9, 13–14
Heym, Stefan 63
High Commission 17
Hiroshima 80
Historians' Dispute 82
Hitler, Adolf 6, 11, 17–19, 22–4, 41, 79, 81, 83, 85
Holocaust Memorial 84, 93
Holocaust (TV series) 82
Honecker, Erich 4, 44–5, 48, 50–1, 53–4, 57, 61–3, 65, 75, 86
Höpcke, Klaus 59
Horn, Gyula 62
Hungary 62, 75
Hurd, Douglas 64

Immigration 1, 7
Initiative for Peace and Human Rights (IFM) 49, 51–2
Iran 7
Israel 80, 82–3

Janka, Walter 47
Jewish Claims Conference 80

Kaiser, Jakob 33
Kennon, George 32
Keßler, Heinz 87
Khrushchev, Nikita 42
Kiel Canal 11
Kiesinger, Georg 43
Kinkel, Klaus 88
Kohl, Helmut 45, 62, 64–7, 68, 72, 82, 84, 88
Köppe, Ingrid 89
Kosovo crisis 93
Krenz, Egon, 61, 63, 65, 88
Krüger, Hans 40

Lafontaine, Oskar 67, 74
League of Culture for the Democratic Renewal of Germany 25–7, 29
Lenin, Vladimir 30
Liberal Democratic Party of Germany (LDPD) 26–7
Liebknecht, Karl 58
London Conference of Foreign Ministers (1947) 25–6
Lower Saxony 13–14
Luxemburg, Rosa 58

Maastricht Treaty 75
Macmillan, Harold 37
Maidanek trials 82
Maizière, Lothar de 65
Mannheim, Karl 20
Marcuse, Herbert 47
Marshall Aid Plan 16, 22, 34
Masur, Kurt 63
McCloy, John 35
Mecklenburg-West Pomerania 4, 7–9, 13, 25, 66, 72, 87
Mielke, Erich 60
Mitterand, François 66
Modrow, Hans 65
Molotov, Vyacheslav 36
Momper, Walter 69

Nagasaki 80
National Democratic Party of Germany (NDPD) 24, 26–7
National Front of a Democratic Germany 26, 29
National Socialism 10, 18, 21, 27, 40, 79–89
Nemeth, Niklos 62
Neuengamme 82, 85
New Forum 62
Nolte, Ernst 82
North Atlantic Treaty Organisation (NATO) 7, 17, 31, 36, 44–5, 50, 66, 77, 91, 93
North Rhine-Westfalia 13–14, 21, 89
Nuremberg Trials 80

Ollenhauer, Erich 37

Organization for European
   Economic Cooperation (OEEC)
   16–17
Ortleb, Rainer 72
Ostpolitik 10, 38, 43–6, 52, 82

Paris Conference of Foreign
   Ministers 32
Paris Treaties 17, 36–7
Parliamentary Council 17–19
Party of Democratic Socialism
   (PDS) 1, 5, 8–9, 64–5, 67, 75,
   77–8, 93
People's Chamber 26–30, 59
People's Congress Movement 25–6
Pöhl, Karl Otto 71
Poland 7, 12, 16, 40, 44, 57, 75, 82
Politburo (GDR) 30, 58, 61–3, 65
Potsdam Conference 12, 13, 23–4,
   32, 34
Prussia 13

Rau, Johannes 89
Ravensbrück 58, 85
Reich, Jens 62
Reuter, Ernst 34
Rhineland-Palatinate 13
Robertson, Brian 35
Roosevelt, Theodore 11
Rügen 70
Rumania 43, 61

Saarland 2
Sachsenhausen 58, 80, 83
Saxony 1, 13, 25, 61–2, 66
Saxony-Anhalt 6–9, 13, 66, 71–2, 87
Schabowski, Günter 88
Schalck-Golodkowski, Alexander 89
Schäuble, Wolfgang 89
Schleswig-Holstein 4, 13–14
Schmidt, Helmut 44–5, 88
Schröder, Gerhard 94
Schumacher, Kurt 14, 33
Schumpeter, Joseph 20
Serbia 7, 93
Silesia 7
Slansky trial 83
Slovenia 7

Social Democratic Party (SPD) 5,
   7–9, 14–15, 21–2, 24, 36, 43–6, 50,
   65, 67, 74–6, 80, 89, 91
Socialist Unity Party (SED) 1, 24–7,
   29–30, 33, 38, 44, 47–8, 50–1,
   52–6, 58–65, 82–5, 87–8, 90
Sokolowski, Marshall 13
Soviet Military Administration
   (SMA) 23, 25
Soviet Union 11–15, 23–30, 32–41,
   44–5, 49, 66–7, 79–80, 82
Späth, Lothar 73
Stalin, Joseph 11, 32, 34–6, 38, 42
Stalinism 10, 25, 41, 64, 80, 82, 88
Stasi 60, 85–7
Stauffenberg, Claus von 85
Stoph, Willi 44
Strauß, Franz Josef 45
Sudetenland 7

Teheran Conference (1943) 11
Thatcher, Margaret 6, 66
Thuringia 13, 25, 66, 71, 74, 90
Tito, Marshall 45
Treaty of Moscow 44
Treaty of Rome 31
Treaty of Warsaw 44
Truman doctrine 16, 34
Trust Holding Company 70–1, 73
Turkey 7

Ulbricht, Walter 23, 27, 45, 53–4, 86
UNESCO (United Nations
   Educational, Scientific and
   Cultural Organization) 44
Unification (of Germany): accession
   of GDR by Basic Law 67; attitude of Adenauer 35–7; co-existence of FRG and GDR 43–6;
   coming to terms with GDR past
   10, 84–9; economic and currency
   union 65–6; economic aspects
   70–7; educational aspects 71;
   German Unity Fund 74; ideas of
   GDR opposition movement
   49–52; move towards in 1989/1990
   63–7; People's Congress
   Movement 25–6; problems of 1–9,
   68–78, 90–3; Stalin's proposals for

36–7; terminological issues 68–70;
Two plus Four negotiations 66;
Unification Treaty 66, 71
United Front of Anti-Fascist and
Democratic Parties 24–5
United Nations Organisation 11
United States of America 11–23,
31–7, 40–1, 44–5, 79–80, 83

Waigel, Theo 75
Warsaw Pact 31, 50, 61
Weimar Republic 18–19, 27

Weiß, Konrad 93
Western European Union (WEU) 31
Wolf, Christa 63
Wurttemberg-Baden 13–14
Wurttemberg-Hohenzollern 13

Yalta Conference 11–12, 51
Yugoslavia 43, 94

'Zonenbeirat' 14